green guide

KANGAROOS AND WALLABIES

···

OF AUSTRALIA

Lee K. Curtis
Series Editor: Louise Egerton

NEW
HOLLAND

First published in 2006 by
New Holland Publishers (Australia) Pty Ltd
Sydney · London · Cape Town · Auckland

14 Aquatic Drive Frenchs Forest NSW 2086 Australia
Garfield House 86 Edgware Road London W2 2EA United Kingdom
80 McKenzie Street Cape Town 8001 South Africa
218 Lake Road Northcote Auckland New Zealand

National Library of Australia Cataloguing-in-Publication Data:

Curtis, Lee, 1957–
Green guide to kangaroos and wallabies of Australia.

Bibliography.
Includes index.
ISBN 1 74110 203 0.

1. Kangaroos - Australia. 2. Wallabies - Australia.
I. Egerton, Louise. II. Title. (Series: Green guide
(New Holland)).

599.220994

Series Editor: Louise Egerton
Project Editor: Yani Silvana
Design: saso content & design pty ltd
Picture Research: Lee Curtis
Production: Grace Gutwein
Printed and bound by: Tien Wah

The body copy is set in 9pt Cheltenham Light.

Photographic Acknowledgments
Abbreviations: NHIL = New Holland Image Library;
Photograph positions: t = top; b = bottom; c = centre; m = main; i = inset; l = left; r = right.

At a Glance: all cover images; pp. 3, 4, 8, 9b, 10–11, 11i, 12t, 13b, 14–15, 16t, 17tl&r, 18–24 (20 painting by Iggi Ronberg of Arrernte tribe), 27i, 28–29, 30t, 31, 32b, 34–35, 36b, 37t, 38t, 39b, 41t, 42t, 43t, 44, 45b, 46–53, 54r, 55b, 57–60, 66, 67b, 70–73, 74b, 75t, 75bl, 76–78, 79b, 80–81, 83t, 84, 87, 88–89, 90b, 91–92, 94–95. **Lochman Transparencies:** Jiri Lochman pp. 7, 17b, 30b, 37b, 45t, 49i, 55t, 68b, 69; Jay Sarson p. 12b; Dennis Sarson p. 54l; H&J Beste pp. 13t, 25b; Dave Watts pp. 5, 26–27, 56, 86.
Bill Corn: 12t, 33t, 33b. **Peter Johnson:** p. 6. **NHIL:** pp. 9t, 16b, 36t, 38b, 39t, 41i, 64t, 75br, 79t, 82, 83b, 85. **By permission of National Library of Australia:** 25t Phillip-Stephan Photo-Litho, 42b painting by H.C. Richter in John Gould's *The Mammals of Australia*, 43b painting in John Gould's *The Mammals of Australia*, 63b, 66t, 67t Photo by D.C. Tilghman, 74t painting by Joseph Lycett.
Malcolm Douglas: 68t. **Tina Janssen:** 31. **Jon Rose:** 32t. **Gary Cranitch, copyright Queensland Museum:** 40. **Greg Eldridge:** 61t, 62t. Darren Jew: 61b, 62b. **Compiled by Rachel J. O'Neill, Professor of Genetics at University of Connecticut:** 64b. **Permission to reproduce the Commonwealth Coat of Arms granted by the Department of the Prime Minister and Cabinet:** 65t. **Australian Rugby Union:** 65b. **ANT Photography:** 89i, 93. **John Young:** 90t

CONTENTS

An Introduction to Kangaroos and Wallabies

Kangaroos and wallabies are native only to Australia and parts of New Guinea. They are marsupials, which means that they are mammals that bear young that are tiny but fully formed. Hairless and blind, the embryonic baby clambers its way into an external womb-like pouch on the belly of its mother. Here it climbs in and attaches itself to one of the teats within. Snug in the pouch, with mother's milk on tap, it will complete its development.

The Bounders

The kangaroo and wallaby family are characterised by their enormous back legs and feet. Instead of running on all fours, they have evolved to hop on these two hindlegs and they are living proof that two legs can be better than four. Among the bigger roos the tail acts as a fifth leg, helping to propel it forward as it jumps. However, when kangaroos and wallabies move slowly over short distances, they use four legs. The front paws hit the ground together and take the roo's weight as it swings the hindlegs beneath its body, its feet landing on either side of the front paws. This is the way grazing kangaroos often move through grasslands.

Hopping is for fast movements. The tail and front paws are lifted off the ground and only the long fourth and small fifth toe, together with the long pad of the bottom of the lower leg, touch the ground. This bounding gait is the one used for quick escapes or long-distance travel.

Claws, Paws and Feet

Kangaroos and wallabies have short thin forearms. Their paws have five clawed digits with which they can hold food efficiently. Roos use their claws to groom and scratch themselves as well as to unearth food morsels.

The back feet have only four toes, each with a claw. Over time the first digit has disappeared completely. The second and third digits have become fused, except for the claws, which are now handy grooming tools. The fourth toe has become enormous and is tipped with a strong claw sometimes used as a weapon. It is from this digit's large padded surface that the kangaroo bounds. The fifth digit is short and undeveloped.

The typical toes and claws on the back feet of bounding kangaroos and wallabies.

> **BIG FOOT**
> Kangaroos and wallabies belong to a family known as macropods. *Macro* is Latin for 'big' and *pod* for 'foot'. So this is the family of the big foot.

Where Do Kangaroos Live?

Kangaroos live in every type of habitat Australia has to offer—from the dense, lush rainforests of far northern Queensland to the hot, arid deserts of central Australia, down to the squeaky white sandy beaches along the Southern Ocean, up the Western Australian Indian Ocean coast and into the tropics of the Northern Territory.

The homes of kangaroos and wallabies vary tremendously. Most animals are nocturnal, coming out to feed and socialise at night. During the day they rest: tree-kangaroos spend most of their time in tropical rainforest treetops; rock-wallabies hide in rocky crevices and fissures; hare-wallabies make tunnels in spinifex hummocks; Bridled Nailtail Wallabies seek refuge in hollowed-out tree trunks; Agile Wallabies fashion caves out of tall grass; and Swamp Wallabies prefer the cover of thick undergrowth in woodlands.

What Kangaroos Eat

Kangaroos and wallabies are herbivores. They mostly eat grasses, herbs and roots. Some are browsers, but others are grazers equipped with highly specialised teeth. Kangaroos mainly eat fibrous grasses whereas wallabies eat more tender leafy plant material. Roos with fine narrow incisors eat short thin grasses while those with bigger teeth eat tall thick grasses. Pademelons, tree-kangaroos and swamp wallabies also eat rainforest leaves and fruit.

How Many Roos and Wallabies Are There?

When European settlers arrived in Australia there were 49 species of kangaroos and wallabies. Two hundred years later there are only 45. Many of those are now on the brink of extinction and some exist only as island populations. Several species once thought to be extinct have resurfaced and other 'new' ones have been discovered thanks to modern DNA studies showing genetic differences not previously recognised.

Surprisingly little is known about kangaroos and wallabies because of their elusive nature and rugged habitats. Most species are a challenge to study in the wild and funding for research is minimal.

Note: Unless otherwise specified, the kangaroo measurements in this book refer to the length of the animal's head and body, not counting the tail.

> **ALL SHAPES AND SIZES**
> Red Kangaroos have been recorded measuring over 2m high and weighing up to 90kg. The Monjon Rock-wallaby, on the other hand, averages 32cm in height and weighs approximately 1.25kg, almost 50 times smaller than the big Red.

What's So Special About Teeth?

*F*or kangaroos and wallabies the type, number and arrangement of their teeth is a major way in which species are identified and relationships between one another understood.

The front cutting teeth are the incisors. There are six in the upper jaw packed together to form a continuous sharp cutting edge in a tight curve. These overlap two much larger, forward-pointing incisors on the bottom jaw that grind against a tough plate on the roof of the mouth.

Between these front teeth and the four pair of back molars is a gap. Once the incisors have cut up the vegetation, the lips and tongue move the food back to be chewed by the molars.

Mighty Molars

In kangaroos, the molars do not appear all at once. Instead, they grow slowly, one pair at a time. As the animal gets older, the skull grows and the front molars wear down and fall out. The rear molars then move forward to replace them. Scientists can tell a roo's age by calculating the degree to which the molars have moved forward.

Most roo species have four pairs of molars and young animals often have a fifth pre-molar at the front of the molars. These successively drop out and move forward. When the last pair wears down, the animal can no longer chew its food and so it dies.

The diet of many large roos consists mostly of fibrous and abrasive grasses. The molars spread the wear and they are deeply ridged to withstand erosion. Wallabies eat more tender leafy plant material so they only need their molars to crush their food. Browsers have a large first premolar that is specially adapted to shearing food. In grazers, this tooth is smaller and lost early in life.

Scientists believe that 40 000 years ago, roo teeth were a third bigger than today.

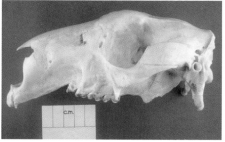

Side view of adult Red Kangaroo skull. Note the gap between the incisors at the front and the molars at the back. The food is cut by the incisors, then passed back to the molars for chewing.

Upper half of skull viewed from underneath. As the kangaroo ages, the front molars wear down and the rear ones move forward as the skull grows larger.

What Makes a Kangaroo a Wallaby?

*I*t's all about size. The big guys are the kangaroos—such as the Reds, Greys and the wallaroos. Any species under 20kg is a wallaby. These smaller species include rock-wallabies, Quokkas, pademelons, nailtail wallabies, hare-wallabies, the Banded Hare-wallaby, tree-kangaroos and the Swamp Wallaby. The smallest is the Monjon Rock-wallaby.

In this book, when speaking generally, all macropods, big or little, are referred to as kangaroos.

What's a Browser and What's a Grazer?

A grazer eats plants that are low, such as grass, ground covers and weeds. A browser eats taller plants, such as shrubs, bushes and leaves off trees.

Larger kangaroos are grazers that specialise in eating grass. Medium-sized species are both browsers and grazers. Smaller species are omnivorous, but they rely on high-quality foods such as nuts, flowers and fungi.

How Do We Know About Roos?

*W*e know how many Australians there are and where and how old they are because every four years a census of the population is conducted. Adults fill out forms answering heaps of questions about what, when, where and how they live, with whom, what they do, etc.

Kangaroos and wallabies can't fill out forms of course but in order to make sure that populations are well and thriving, we need to learn as much as possible about them. So scientists sometimes catch animals and measure, weigh and examine them carefully. They may even take blood samples or equip them with radio collars before letting them go. The information gathered is then fed into computers or analysed by statisticians. This gives scientists a fairly accurate estimate of populations and other important facts and figures about various species.

'Oh, it's at least a foot.' A scientist measuring a rock-wallaby's foot in the field.

Why Hop When You Can Walk?

*K*angaroos' large, powerful hindlegs are often compared to springs, pogo sticks and rubber balls. All store elastic energy that is effortlessly renewed with every bounce (or hop). Hopping is actually a surprisingly energy-efficient mode of transportation. There are two reasons for this.

Two hopping Reds: one going up, the other down.

Firstly, in roos and wallabies the spring action is carried out by the Achilles tendons, which attach the heel muscles to the calf muscles, and tendons expend less effort than muscles. Secondly, this mode of travel is enhanced by a phenomenon likened to the workings of an internal piston. Each time a kangaroo's big hind feet leave the ground, the diaphragm moves up and air is pushed out of the lungs. When the kangaroo lands, the suction caused by the downward pressure of the internal organs on the diaphragm causes air to be pulled in. The combination of these two mechanisms means that when a kangaroo hops at high speeds, it uses up less energy and oxygen than animals that run or gallop.

Why Is Energy Efficiency So Important?

*M*any kangaroos live surrounded by plentiful supplies of food but others must travel incredibly long distances every day through deserts, sparse scrub or rocky territory to locate food, so conserving energy is important.

Survival depends largely on being able to move away from danger quickly and efficiently. Escaping predators is also a constant challenge. Prior to the arrival of Europeans, the only predators on macropods for thousands of years were Aboriginal people, Dingos, Wedge-tailed Eagles and large pythons. Today the domestic dog, foxes and the white man's shotguns represent even greater threats.

Being able to escape from predators is a key to macropod survival.

ROOS ON A TREADMILL

Unlike a running dog or galloping horse, kangaroos use less energy the faster they go. Scientific studies carried out using treadmills have shown that a kangaroo maintains a constant number of hops per minute. If the treadmill speeds up, the roo just takes longer and longer hops.

How Sensitive Are Roo Senses?

This Eastern Grey sniffs the air to check for danger.

*F*rom day one, roos and wallabies have a remarkable sense of smell. The tiny, fully formed first-born clambers from its mother's opening under her tail up through a forest of fur with the sharp little claws of its forearm and only its sense of smell to guide it safely into mum's life-saving pouch.

Smell is a vital clue to so much of a roo's world. Smells can forecast danger and changing weather conditions and they provide information about fellow roos. Males spend a lot of time sniffing at pouches and under females' tails trying to ascertain whether a female is ready to mate.

Kangaroos and wallabies also have very good eyesight and they respond particularly well to moving things. The eyes are located on the side of their heads and guarantee the animal a wide field of vision. Their night vision is excellent, too.

Sonar ears

Roos have an extremely keen sense of hearing. Not only can they turn their ears independently, which allows them to hear noises coming from different directions, but they can also turn their ears 180°. It is rare to see a kangaroo or wallaby with immobile ears; even when at rest their ears are twitching, constantly alert.

This Antilopine is listening to noises coming from different directions.

DROUGHT-PROOF ROOS?
Scientists estimate that a kangaroo needs the same amount of water as a camel—about one-quarter the amount that sheep and cattle require. A roo does not have to drink water if it can get it from the vegetation it eats. Losing up to 20% of its body weight during droughts will not harm it.

LARGE KANGAROOS

What Is an Alpha Male?

*T*he alpha male is usually the biggest and strongest kangaroo in a mob. This dominant male has fought for, and won, his position. He is the leader, the main teacher and the primary breeder. Females prefer to mate with him over any other male. Breeding females instinctively know he will provide good genes for future generations.

Once he has attained the top position in a mob, the alpha male must constantly watch out for potential challengers and be willing to defend his status—aggressively if necessary. He will only lose this status when a stronger, if not younger, male stands up to him and wins the fight.

Standing tall and proud: this alpha male Red Kangaroo stands almost 2m high.

How Do Male Kangaroos Establish Dominance?

*W*hen a kangaroo has exhausted all non-violent methods of directing a rival male's attention away from his intended, he may resort to physical force in order to assert his dominance. He approaches his adversary and stands up tall in front of him as if to say, 'Okay, Mate, you're going to have to go through me to get at my girl'. If ignored, the challenger starts to pretend smack or paw his rival. When this fails to provoke a response he either hops away or finds something else to do—like chew on some grass or groom himself. If the contender accepts the challenge, the kangaroos face each other and stand on their tip-toes to attain their maximum height. Most of the time they just stand there and stare at each other until one gives up. Rarely do they resort to blows. When they do, however, the display is impressive.

These two wannabe boomers are sizing each other up.

WHAT'S A BOOMER?
A boomer is a big male Red or Grey Kangaroo.

Are Kangaroos Dangerous?

*T*here have been few reports of kangaroos hurting humans but if they do, there is usually a logical explanation. A male kangaroo courting a female, for example, does not appreciate company, be it human or kangaroo. If you approach a 'male on a mission' he may feel challenged. If he stands tall, and puffs his chest out and starts making boxing gestures, back off immediately or be prepared to suffer the consequences.

Another occasion when it is unwise to butt in is when two male kangaroos are sparring; you may get in the firing line. Females, too, can get nasty with a fellow roo or human that comes near her young joey. Another flashpoint may be when kangaroos that are accustomed to being fed by people become demanding and even aggressive.

Do Kangaroos Really Box?

*Y*ou bet they do. But full-fledged fights occur only between two males of similar size and strength. With their heads bent back to avoid getting their eyes clawed, they lash out at each other with their front paws. If this doesn't work, they'll lean back on their tails and give their rival a mighty powerful kick in the stomach with their huge feet. Fights don't usually last more than a few minutes and the loser concedes by turning away and ignoring his challenger.

Wallabies, except for Agiles, don't use their tails for support. They jump at their opponents instead.

Injuries are seldom more serious than a few gashes, bruises and scratches.

What Is a Mob?

*L*arge kangaroos often like to hang out together in groups of 10 or more, sometimes up to hundreds, called mobs. The Eastern and Western Grey Kangaroo and the Antilopine are particularly social, while Red Kangaroos generally stick together in groups of about four. The Euro is the least social of the large kangaroos along with the Black Wallaroo.

A mob of Grey Kangaroos graze peaceably out in the open but within bounding distance of dense vegetation.

Eastern Grey Kangaroo

Eastern Grey Kangaroos live in the eastern parts of the continent, including on the inland plains, on the Great Dividing Range and along the coast wherever sufficient fresh water is available.

Males can reach up to 2m in height and weigh up to 66kg, whereas females are about half this size. Being sociable animals, these roos live together in mobs of

This large Eastern Grey Kangaroo is the alpha male of his group. His excellent genes will ensure a healthy future for his species.

ten or more individuals. In charge is usually an older, dominant male. His position is attained by winning fighting bouts with other males and it is he that usually sires the offspring of fertile females in the mob. Females are ready to mate at 18 months but males don't reach sexual maturity for two years.

You can identify Eastern Greys by their furry muzzles and their dark tail tips. Coat colours are grey or brown but shades vary. Those on the coast are usually lighter in colour than their darker inland counterparts. However, both tend to have relatively pale fronts.

■ *Western Grey*
  Eastern Grey
■ *Overlap*

Eastern Greys eat grasses and broad-leaved herbaceous plants. Prior to the arrival of Europeans, they are believed to have mostly inhabited woodland and forested areas which perhaps explains why they are much more prone to dehydration than the more plains-orientated Red Kangaroos. When white people began to build dams for their domestic stock on arid properties, however, the Greys moved into drier territory.

Forester Kangaroos

The Eastern Greys found in Tasmania are known as Forester Kangaroos. To withstand the icy winters they have thicker fur than their mainland cousins and it is darker in colour. They are also slightly smaller. Forester Kangaroos are a protected species in Tasmania. Their population is restricted to the north-eastern and central parts of the State.

Western Grey Kangaroo

Despite differences in colouring, both of these animals are from Western Australia. The white blaze on the forehead is frequently seen on Western Greys.

Until the 1970s, the Western Grey was thought to be merely a subspecies of the Eastern Grey. Telling the difference between the two is not easy. Both are similar in size and build: Western males are up to 2m long and weigh up to 66kg; larger females are 1m long and weigh 28kg. Westerns tend to have a dark brown head and back with greyish blue fur on the front. That said, there is considerable variability across their range which extends over most of the

> **STINKAROO**
> Western Greys also go by the names of Black-faced Kangaroos, Mallee Kangaroos and 'stinkers' (because of their pungent curry-like odour).

southern half of the continent, stopping right before the Great Dividing Range in the east. As a general rule, those in the west are browner, leaner animals compared with the stockier, greyer eastern roos. Confusingly, the home ranges of Eastern and Western Greys overlap on the plains of central and western New South Wales as well as western Victoria and south-eastern South Australia.

The major differences between Eastern and Western Greys appears to lie in the duration of their respective reproductive cycles. Western Greys have shorter pregnancies, shorter times for joeys in the pouch and generally shorter reproductive cycles than their eastern counterparts.

How Kangaroo Island Got Its Name

Perhaps surprisingly the first specimen of the Western Grey to be collected more than a century before it was identified as such came from an island off the coast of South Australia known today as Kangaroo Island. The island was named by the famous explorer, Matthew Flinders, who landed there in 1805. He named it after the impressive abundance of Grey kangaroos that lived there and seemed unafraid of humans. Flinders' men took advantage of this trust and proceeded to slaughter them for meat. The Kangaroo Island animals are now recognised as a separate subspecies from those on the mainland.

How Does a Roo Woo?

When a female kangaroo is ready to breed, large males take a keen interest in her. Although courting practices in some species are more complex than others, the basics are the same. The dominant male follows the female around, occasionally sniffs her and makes sure that other potential suitors do not interfere.

The male can tell when the female is ready to mate by the way she smells. This female still has a joey in her pouch so he will have to be patient a while longer.

As breeding time draws near, the male may gently paw at his intended's head, sniff at her pouch and, as is common among many male mammals, grab the base of her tail with his paws. Sometimes a male will stand tall in front of the female showing off his erect penis. Others will grab the female's head and rub it against their chest. Males often make tender clucking sounds and sniff at her under-tail, awaiting that special odour that signals the time for mating is nigh. Flirting males also bob their heads up and down. If the male gets too carried away before the time is right, the female makes a sharp throaty coughing noise to shoo her wooer away.

Is It a Private Affair?

No. Roos don't get any privacy during copulation. Even while mating, the dominant male may have to aggressively fight off other interested males. This is an admirable feat considering he is standing halfway upright behind his mate who is crouched down while he hugs her around the waist with his paws. With various interruptions and rest periods, intercourse can take up to an hour.

The female of most roo species is ready to mate one or two days after giving birth.

When Is a Tail a Leg?

*T*he tails of the large kangaroos and wallabies are long, strong, muscular and tapered at the end. They are used as rudders and for balance when bounding across terrain. They also provide additional support when a kangaroo sits down. Another service provided by a roo's tail is to act as a prop when the animal moves its hind legs forward while grazing on all fours—or fives. Importantly, too, for males is the tail as a

In slow mode roos use heir tails as a third hindleg.

support, or extra leg, during fights. When a male attempts to kick his opponent with his hind legs, the tail must carry the roo's entire weight.

Leaning back on their tails, males can kick forward with both hindlegs together.

What's a Wallaroo?

*W*allaroos are usually large, stocky roos with broad chests. Their characteristic stance sets them apart from other large kangaroos and wallabies. The muscular body is held more vertically and they also hop more upright. The shoulders are pulled close into the chest. The forelimbs are large and well developed but the paws are usually turned down so the wrists and knuckles face forward.

There are three species of wallaroo: Common Wallaroo, Black Wallaroo and Antilopine Wallaroo. Most live in mountainous and rocky regions of continental Australia, where caves and rock

Euros are a type of Common Wallaroo. This family lives in rugged arid coastal Western Australia.

ledges provide shelter from extreme temperatures. During the day they rest hidden in the deep shadows afforded by gorges and gaps between rocks, protected from predators. In the cool of the evening they venture out onto the slopes to graze on grasses and browse on low bushes.

Red Kangaroos

The largest living marsupial in the world is the Red Kangaroo. Its Latin name, *Macropus rufus*, is Latin for 'red big foot'. The males are solid, handsome animals that can stand over 2m tall and weigh up to 90kg. Females are less than half the size and weigh 25–40kg. Reds continue to grow throughout most of their life.

The dominant fur colour among males is usually pinkish brown to deep rusty red but sometimes they are bluish or reddish grey. Whatever the colouring, it is usually unevenly distributed. The underside, hindlegs, forearms and tail tips are lighter

This adult male watches over his female mate who is half his size. Reds live 15–18 years in the wild.

in colour but their toes and paws are dark. Females most often have blue–grey fur and are called blue-fliers.

Reds are the most numerous species of roos and wallabies in Australia. Numbers have been known to exceed 8 million but populations fluctuate drastically depending on weather conditions. This is one of the species that is regularly culled for the kangaroo industry.

Where Reds Live

Reds are widespread in central Australia and live in every Territory and State except Tasmania. They prefer open, grassy plains with occasional shade trees but are also found in mallee, saltbush and mulga country, low open woodlands and even in deserts. Despite their preference for drier regions, they are quite partial to green grass and herbs.

While most Reds are sedentary animals that settle in one area, some—particularly mature adults—are nomadic and will travel long distances. Why they do this is not fully understood but movement is common during times of drought when they must travel far afield to find food.

> **TELLING TAILS**
> Reds have light-coloured or white-tipped tails. Greys' tails have dark tips.

Common Wallaroo

An adult (above) and juvenile (right) Western Wallaroo.

The male Common Wallaroo stands up to 1.9m high and weighs 55kg. It is a big, robust kangaroo with large, muscular forearms, a broad chest and paws that tuck under. Females are only half the size. The colouring of its coarse shaggy coat, which is always paler on the underside, varies from region to region. Its characteristic stocky build is well suited to the rocky country it generally inhabits.

Common Wallaroos may breed at any time of year but if conditions become difficult breeding will cease until they improve. Females are ready to mate after one and half to two years. Their pregancy lasts about a month and young may remain in the pouch for over eight months.

The Four Types of Common Wallaroo

Four different types of Common Wallaroo have evolved from four distinct geographical regions.

Perhaps the best known is the Euro, which lives in dry rugged regions of central New South Wales and Queensland, all the way across the continent to the Indian Ocean. Euros are tough animals with thick padding on the hopping part of their hindlegs. From east to west their colouring varies from a dark brown to a rich red. Much of their diet consists of spiky spinifex grass or saltbush. Because they have the ability to conserve their own body fluids they rarely need to drink but, with the provision of dams in the outback, Euros have colonised regions previously too arid even for them.

ROCKY ROOS
'Wallaroo' is an Aboriginal word for 'rock-wallaby'.

The Eastern Wallaroo that inhabits the Great Dividing Range has a very dark, coarse coat. That of the Western is generally an orangey red. The male Northern Wallaroo tends to be red, while the female is greyer. The Barrow Island Wallaroo, cut off from the mainland for about 13 000 years, is smaller than its mainland counterparts.

What Is a Totem?

*T*he Aborigines identify with plants, animals and other natural elements. Each newborn child is assigned a totem. A kangaroo or wallaby totem means that the person is responsible for the animal's wellbeing throughout their lifetime. It is the Aboriginal way of ensuring the survival of the species.

Who Is Malu?

*K*angaroos and wallabies have been an important part of Aboriginal life for thousands of years—perhaps as many as 50 000. In the old days, besides providing Aborigines with food, kangaroo and wallaby skins were used to make clothing and blankets; bones, sinew and assorted other animal body parts produced needles, tools, musical instruments and weapons. Strangely enough, despite the fact that Aborigines eat kangaroos and wallabies, these animals are prominently featured in their Dreamtime and many tribes adopt a species of kangaroo or wallaby as their totem.

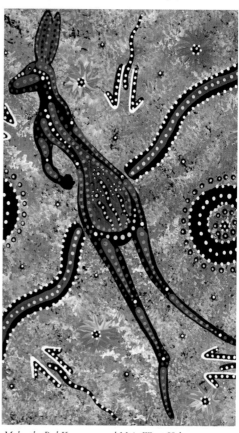

For example, Malu the Red Kangaroo is a totem of the central Australian Arrernte tribes. In this painting by Iggi Ronberg of the Arrernte tribe, the kangaroo follows a trail (two thick squiggly brown and black lines with dots) to reach the water holes (two black circles). The kangaroo's large hind footprints are represented by the black-and-white-spotted tick-shaped lines and the tail's imprint is in between these. The grey flowers represent the spinifex bushes in flower and the little white dots are bush medicines.

Malu, the Red Kangaroo, and Main Water Hole story.

Who Nose?

NOSE PANTING
Kangaroos pant through their noses with their mouths closed.

*F*rom afar it's not easy to tell the difference between Reds, Greys and Wallaroos. But their muzzles will solve the puzzle if you can get close enough to see these clearly.

The Red has very distinctive white patches with black spots and lines on the sides. A wide white stripe runs from the corner of the mouth up to the base of each ear. The tip of the nose is well defined, V-shaped, hairless and blackish grey with a grainy texture. The Grey's muzzle is covered with peach fuzz fur and the nostrils are thin and well defined. Common, Antilopine and Black Wallaroos have a large black triangular, hairless nose tip.

Red Kangaroo   *Grey Kangaroo*   *Wallaroo*

Do Kangaroos Blush?

*B*elieve it or not, both male and female Red Kangaroos 'blush' during the breeding season. This is particularly obvious on the chest and neck of males. The blush is caused by a red powdery substance secreted by the animals themselves.

The substance, known as cinnabarinic acid, is also found in red mushrooms and it is thought to be responsible for the strange colouring around the head and neck of the Purple-necked Rock-wallaby, as well as the orange tint that appears on the upper inner thighs of Lumholtz's Tree-kangaroo.

The bright red–orange colouring on breeding Red males sometimes covers the entire neck and chest.

Black Wallaroo

'Bark' is a young male wallaroo on display at the Territory Wildlife Park, Berry Springs, NT.

A macho Black Wallaroo—solitary and mostly nocturnal.

The Black Wallaroo lives **only** on the isolated sandstone plateau and rocky escarpments of Arnhem Land. Solitary and mostly nocturnal, it is a bit of a mystery to scientists. It has never been found in a group bigger than three. We know that it spends the day in caves and under rocky overhangs and that it feeds in the cool of the night and early morning on grasses and small shrubs. To find out more, studies are currently underway.

With the exception of the Barrow Island Wallaroo, the Black Wallaroo is the smallest of the large kangaroos, measuring around 73cm and weighing 13–22kg. Despite its name, many animals, especially females and immature males, are sooty grey, although breeding males are usually pitch black with a tinge of orange on their forearms.

Conservation Worries

Because the Black Wallaroo is only known to exist in remote areas, efforts are being made to start a breeding program at the Territory Wildlife Park near Darwin. It is feared that should the existing populations succumb to an epidemic, say a virus, the entire population could be lost and this would be the end of a species. Another big worry for the Black Wallaroo is the destruction of its habitat and its food by the recent practice of burning off valuable grasslands too frequently.

To learn more about how this roo lives, scientists are consulting with local Aboriginal people, whose knowledge of the animals may flesh out the limited understanding we currently have. In so doing wildlife managers will be more qualified to help manage Black Wallaroo populations and so to ensure their survival.

Antilopine Wallaroo

Although related to walla-roos, the Antilopine is a tropical member not restricted to the usual rocky terrain of wallaroos. Instead it has adapted to the flat grassy plains and savanna woodlands of northern Australia. It roams across the Kimberley in the west and over the Top End to central Cape York. Although Antilopine populations are separated by the Gulf of Carpentaria, there is no evidence of genetic differences, which indicates that they do travel and mix.

The Top End's largest kangaroos, male Antilopines, stand up to 1.2m; females reach 84cm. They weigh up to 49 and 20kg respectively. The shape of the male's head is similar to that of the Red's but with a more bulbous nose, and the ears are trimmed with light-coloured fur. The male's coat is red and tan above with a white underside. The female varies in colour, generally with a pale grey head and a red and/or tan back like the males. The tips of Antilopine paws and hind feet are black.

Not exactly the Brad Pitt of macropods, this big-nosed kangaroo is very gregarious.

This species is leaner than typical wallaroos and it behaves more like the Red and Grey Kangaroos. Perhaps that is why it is sometimes referred to as the Antilopine Kangaroo.

A Social Roo

It is the most social of all the large kangaroos, living in groups of up to eight individuals run by a dominant male. When threatened, groups form mobs of 30 or more animals. Antilopines groom one another, an uncommon practice among kangaroos. When annoyed, they grunt loudly.

During the wet season the Antilopine is active during the day as well as at night. It breeds year-round but most births occur at the end of the wet season.

Can You Tell a Roo by its Hop?

*K*angaroo and wallaby experts pride themselves on being able to tell the difference between the larger kangaroos by their hopping styles.

The Red holds its head low in line with its flat back. The tail is held straight and swings only slightly. The Eastern Grey keeps its forearms low, back flat and head up. When it hops quickly, its tail arches upwards and swings up and down. The Western Grey's style is very similar but it holds its head lower and steadier than the Eastern Grey.

Eastern Greys like this one keep their forearms low, their back flat and their head up while hopping.

Wallaroos stand more erect when hopping, their backs at a 45° angle to the horizon. They hold their forearms close to their body and take shorter hops than the other big roos. On flat, open land wallaroos might appear ungainly compared to Greys and Reds but they navigate nimbly across their hilly home territory.

What's Bigger than a Big Red?

*W*hen Europeans first arrived in Australia, the Red Kangaroo was the biggest mammal on the continent. With the settlers came exotic animals that pushed the kangaroo down the list to the thirteenth largest behind introduced buffalos, cattle, horses, donkeys, camels, pigs and five kinds of deer.

The fact that the kangaroo industry pays roo shooters per kilo encourages hunters to go after the largest animals first. As a result the biggest Reds, reported to measure over 3m in height as recently as the 1960s, no longer exist.

The Big Red is no longer the king of Australian land mammals.

Who Were the First Conservationists?

*T*he Krantji Kangaroo clan—northern Arrernte Aboriginal people of central Australia—trace their spiritual lineage to their totem, the Red Kangaroo. The Krantji hunt Red Kangaroos for food, but hunting is allowed only in certain areas that are chosen based on ancient myths and traditions passed down through the generations.

A recent study revealed that the locations where hunting is prohibited correspond almost exactly to areas of prime Red Kangaroo habitat. This effectively means that the Krantji have conservation reserves for the Red Kangaroo to prevent it being over hunted. The practical application of the Krantji's spiritual beliefs to their everyday interactions with nature ensures the ongoing survival of their people, their major food source and the environment.

For thousands of years Aboriginal people have hunted kangaroos sustainably.

Can Kangaroos Swim?

*K*angaroos and wallabies are perfectly good swimmers. Although this is not an activity they undertake often, when under duress, particularly when being chased by a predator such as a dog or Dingo, kangaroos will not hesitate to jump in the water. Hot days are also an incentive to go for a dip.

Strangely enough, the roo propels itself in the water by moving its rear legs independently of each other, something it cannot do on land. By tightening the muscles around her pouch and sealing it, a mother roo can swim and keep her joey safe and dry.

> **DROWNING DOGS**
> Dogs have often been observed chasing kangaroos into water. If the dog is determined and pursues the roo into the water, it will more than likely regret it. The roo will grab hold of the dog's head with its sharp-clawed forepaws and hold it under water for as long as it takes.

WALLABIES & NAILTAILS

Agile Wallaby

A fully grown male Agile Wallaby stands about 1.4m high and weighs up to 27kg; the female is about half this size. This sandy brown wallaby has a characteristic pale thigh stripe. Black-bordered white facial stripes run parallel from the nose to and past the eyes respectively.

Like the bigger kangaroos, the Agile Wallaby uses its large tail as a fifth leg, for balance and for support when fighting and lashing out with its hindlegs. When hopping, it holds its arms out straight in front and holds its head high.

In profile the face of this elegant wallaby has a sort of Roman-nose appearance. Its forearms are exceptionally long and its paws remarkably dexterous. It can handle objects much like humans, and males have been observed 'climbing' their intended mate's tail, hand over hand, from the tip to the base. Indeed, so nimble-handed is this wallaby that it is able to fashion a cave-like shelter out of long grasses, where it rests during the day.

Note the unusually long arms.

A nimble-handed Agile shows off his Roman nose.

Where to Find Them

The Agile Wallaby lives in open forests and grasslands near fresh water. It digs up native grasses to munch on the roots and it digs holes to find drinking water. It is an opportunistic eater—a grazer as well as a browser—that will gladly nibble away on young paperbarks, low shrubs and even Leichhardt tree fruit and native figs. Its habit of uprooting grasses in agricultural areas sometimes earns it the label of pest.

Social creatures, Agiles move around in groups of up to 10 animals. Where food is abundant, larger numbers congregate. It is the most commonly seen wallaby in the wet tropics of northern Australia, including in Kakadu National Park and on Queensland's east coast.

IN NEW GUINEA, TOO

Apart from the Red-legged Pademelon, the Agile Wallaby is the only Australian wallaby to be also found in New Guinea.

Tammar Wallaby

The Tammar Wallaby, also referred to as the Dama Wallaby, was the first kangaroo to be sighted and recorded by a European, François Pelsaert, who was shipwrecked on the Abrohlos Islands off the coast of Western Australia.

Large numbers of Tammars used to live in the coastal regions of south-western Australia and parts of South Australia, including Kangaroo Island. The mainland Tammar, however, was virtually wiped out by land clearing, foxes, dogs and cats. There are a few in South Australia and perhaps some in remote regions of Western Australia.

One of the smallest macropods, it measures no more than 65cm and weighs less than

The largest population of Tammars lives on Kangaroo Island, off the coast of South Australia.

10kg. It is a lovely chunky wallaby with thick, light grey–brown fur and rufous highlights on its hindlegs and forearms. When it hops, it holds these forearms well apart.

Surviving Times of Drought

Tammar Wallabies living on Kangaroo Island often have to go without water for months. In these times of drought, they appear to be able to drink sea water. Some scientists believe that what they are actually doing is skimming a layer of fresh water off the top of the sea. In the absence of turbulence, fresh water floats on the surface of salt-laden sea water. This theory would explain why these animals are able to maintain a healthy weight on their diet of dry grass.

A nocturnal animal, the Tammar spends the day resting under the dense cover of the coastal scrub. It is a seasonal breeder with births occurring between January and March. The female reaches sexual maturity at nine months. At this time she may still be in her mum's pouch and suckling. The term of a Tammar's pregnancy is the shortest of all the kangaroos: on average 28.3 days.

NOVELTY DAMAS
'Damas' or Tammar Wallabies are a favourite to breed in captivity and they are one of the most studied species of kangaroos because scientists see them as a 'typical' macropod.

Do Roos Ever Escape From Captivity?

*I*n 1926 a pair of Brush-tailed Rock-wallabies escaped from a private fauna collection on the island of Oahu, Hawaii, and sought refuge in the nearby Kalihi Mountains. Today it is believed that their descendants form a colony of up to 100 animals.

On display: a Red-necked Wallaby takes it easy.

In the 1930s and 40s, Red-necked (Bennett's) and Tammar Wallabies escaped from various collections and zoos in England and now form several small colonies there. In January 2004 a wild Red-necked Wallaby was discovered in Belgium. Not surprisingly, it was suffering from frostbite.

Can Pests Ever Be Valuable?

*Y*es, they certainly can. One country's pest can be another country's endangered native animal and, as such, vitally important to saving the species.

In the late 1880s a former South Australian and New Zealand Governor shipped Tammar, Parma and Swamp Wallabies, as well as Brush-tailed Rock-wallabies, to his new island home near Auckland, New Zealand. By the 1950s–60s these wallabies had completely destroyed the native vegetation and made it impossible to establish any farms on the island.

Although island residents regularly culled the wallabies or exported them to zoos and wildlife parks, they continued to breed. In 2004 they were declared pests by the New Zealand government.

Prior to the total eradication of the unwelcome wallabies, several conservation and research groups from Australia were able to trap Parma Wallabies and Brush-tailed Rock-wallabies—species that were endangered on mainland Australia—and bring them back to their native home to establish breeding colonies and boost their sadly dwindling populations.

The Parma Wallaby thrives in zoos around the world.

What Makes a Kangaroo Sick?

*K*angaroos and wallabies can get a bacterial infection called 'lumpy jaw'. This causes big abscesses to swell up on the jaw and sometimes the tongue, so that the animal is unable to eat. Lumpy jaw is usually contracted by captive animals and is associated with overcrowding. Often the crust on bread fed to these animals by tourists cuts the gum, providing an entry point for the bacteria. Captive roos have a chance of being cured with antibiotics but in the wild the disease is fatal.

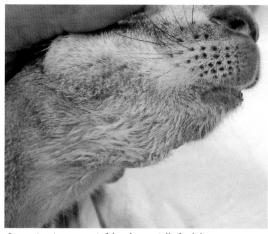

Lumpy jaw is a very painful and potentially fatal disease.

Kangaroos can also get a disease of the intestine called coccidiosis. This comes from a microscopic soil-borne protozoa. The primary symptoms are diarrhoea and weight loss. This disease is very difficult to treat and it is believed that it can remain dormant in the affected animal even after it recovers. Eastern Greys are particularly susceptible to this sickness.

> **IMPORTED PARASITES**
> Three to four thousand years ago, travelling Indonesians brought Dingos to Australia. Unfortunately the animals carried nematodes and tapeworms in their stomachs. They passed these on to kangaroos and wallabies. Although these parasites are not usually fatal, they can make a roo feel rather crook.

How Did Aborigines Catch and Cook Roos?

*T*he Noongar Aboriginal people from southern Western Australia hunted Quokkas and Western Grey Kangaroos sustainably for many centuries. The Noongar caught Quokkas in deep pit traps that they dug and camouflaged with branches and dirt, or they surrounded and speared them, sometimes while burning off the bush.

The most common ways of preparing the meat were to grill strips on the fire or to place it in a hole covered with ashes and a slow burning fire on top. The remaining body parts did not go to waste. The skins were made into clothing or bags. The bones were carved into nose-bones and the sinew used for sewing and binding.

How Did the Dingo Fence Benefit Roos?

*T*he Dingo Fence is the world's longest fence. It was built in the 1880s to protect sheep from their main predator, the Dingo. The fence runs along the border of South Australia and New South Wales, all the way across South Australia, along the New South Wales and Queensland borders and through central Queensland.

Lucky kangaroos on the southern side of the fence lost one of their major predators. Research shows that the population density of kangaroos on that side can be up to 100 times greater than that of the northern side where Dingo numbers remain much higher.

Built to protect domestic animals, the Dingo Fence keeps native animals that are on the south side of it safe as well.

Where Do Roos Go in a Drought?

*R*esearchers estimate that during severe droughts 50–70% of roos in a given region can die.

Larger kangaroos will move in an attempt to find food and water. This often means they infringe on human territory, be it farmland, suburbia or golf courses. They are not always welcome and often considered pests by those who do not understand that the kangaroo is simply doing whatever it takes to survive.

Most small roos perish in a drought.

During a severe drought the toll on kangaroo populations can be devastating.

PICKY EATERS
Although Dingos prefer rabbit to kangaroo, they will not hesitate to go after joeys and old male roos in areas where rabbits and other small animals are scarce, or during a drought.

Why Are Kangaroos Culled?

*K*angaroos are culled to supply meat and skins for the kangaroo industry and for damage mitigation.

Graziers and farmers who are worried that their property is being damaged by an over-abundance of kangaroos can apply for a Damage Mitigation permit. A wildlife ranger will then visit the property in question, assess the situation, and may give the landowner a permit which allows him to kill a certain number of a species. It is the shooter's duty to euthanase any pouch joeys humanely.

The general public are not allowed into areas where kangaroo culling is underway.

In many cases the shooter must leave the carcasses where they fall. They cannot be used for food or any other purpose; this is the law.

How Are Culling Quotas Determined?

*E*ach year State governments report to the Federal government their population estimates of certain species of kangaroos and wallabies. Based on these estimates, the government sets quotas for culling. These generally reflect 10–20% of the total population of a species. The commercial kangaroo harvest quota for 2004 was 4.4 million kangaroos.

Most commonly Reds, Eastern and Western Greys and Common Wallaroos are harvested. Smaller numbers of Whiptail Wallabies, Red-necked Wallabies and Tasmanian Pademelons have also been harvested in the recent past.

In Queensland and New South Wales the quotas are carefully restricted to certain regions to make sure populations are well managed.

In 2003 alone over 3 million Eastern Greys were shot.

KANGAROO FARMS
To date there are no kangaroo farms in Australia. All kangaroo products sold around the world come from kangaroos shot in the wild. Whereas farming wildlife such as deer is an economically viable practice, the challenges of effectively farming kangaroos have yet to be successfully met.

Parma Wallaby

The Parma Wallaby is a pretty little wallaby that grows to a little over half a metre and weighs no more than 6kg. Its fur is a rufous or greyish brown above, grey about the head, fading to pale grey underneath. It has a white stripe along the lower lip that reaches almost to the eye. The tail is blackish, sparsely furred and approximately half a metre long.

Classified as rare or endangered, the Parma lives in wet and dry sclerophyll forests of New South Wales on the Great Dividing Range. This nocturnal animal shelters in shrubs during the day. It constructs runways through these shrubs and emerges to feed on grasses and herbs at night. The Parma can hop very quickly while remaining close to the ground in an almost horizontal position with its forearms stuck close to its body.

When agitated or sexually aroused, the little Parma Wallaby 'wags' the tip or all of its tail.

Mostly solitary, it will feed with other members of its species. If there is enough food available, Parma Wallabies will reproduce year-round.

Pulled from the Brink of Extinction

In 1965 this species was thought to be extinct but fortunately it was one of the wallabies transported to New Zealand by the then South Australian governor. Over the next eight years 300 animals were sent around the world to zoos and, although their numbers remain low in the wild, the Parma Wallaby is now a popular animal in zoos throughout the world.

KANGAROO LANGUAGE

Roos and wallabies are not very vocal animals. The noises they make include guttural hissing, clucking, coughing, snorting and stomping their feet. These sounds are usually made to warn of danger, to beckon young, to flirt, or because a roo is suddenly frightened.

Whiptail Wallaby

The Whiptail Wallaby is believed to be the most populous species of wallaby in Australia and is one of five kangaroo species harvested for commercial purposes

At last, here is a wallaby you can identify at the drop of a hat. Its other name, Pretty Face, gives the clue away. Front-on, the dark face is outlined on each side by a wedge-shaped white cheek stripe that gives this wallaby a distinctive V-shaped face. Seen from the back, the ears are long and tri-coloured with blackish tips and a brown base topped with a wide white stripe. The name 'whiptail' refers to its exceedingly long tail that extends the length of its body and tapers to a slender whip-like end.

The tail tapers to a thin, whip-like end.

Habits and Behaviour

The Whiptail is one of the largest wallabies, averaging 2m including its tail, and weighing 15–27kg. It can hop extremely fast and is able to jump very high. It is also a gregarious roo—groups of six and up to 50 individuals are common. Active by day and night, they graze grasses, ferns and herbs in open woodlands along the coasts of Queensland and northern New South Wales. Competition among males is fierce as breeding females prefer macho males.

When alarmed, a Whiptail thumps its hindfoot to warn the others in the mob. They then all hop off on a zigzag path to avoid their predator. The Whiptail's slow hop is upright but when in a hurry its back and tail are horizontal.

What's So Great About Roo Farts?

*M*ethane is a greenhouse gas and so contributes to global warming. It destroys the protective ozone layer surrounding our planet. Cows can burp up to 250L of methane each day and sheep 25L but Australia's enviromentally friendly roos and wallabies are not significant contributors to global warming because their burps and farts don't contain methane.

When a cow or sheep eats, the food is broken down by bacteria in its stomach. Methane is a waste product of this process. Kangaroo stomachs have special bacteria that break down the nutrients without producing harmful methane, so kangaroo farts are methane free.

They may fart and burp but our number-one native grazers and browsers are zero methane emitters.

How Do Kangaroos Prepare For Birth?

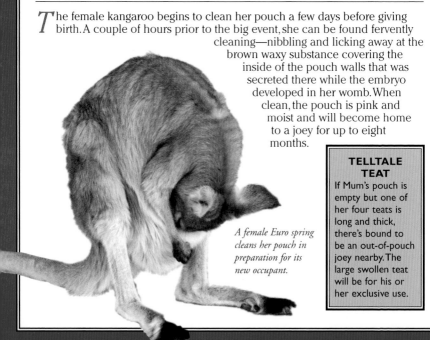

*T*he female kangaroo begins to clean her pouch a few days before giving birth. A couple of hours prior to the big event, she can be found fervently cleaning—nibbling and licking away at the brown waxy substance covering the inside of the pouch walls that was secreted there while the embryo developed in her womb. When clean, the pouch is pink and moist and will become home to a joey for up to eight months.

A female Euro spring cleans her pouch in preparation for its new occupant.

TELLTALE TEAT

If Mum's pouch is empty but one of her four teats is long and thick, there's bound to be an out-of-pouch joey nearby. The large swollen teat will be for his or her exclusive use.

How Do Kangaroos Give Birth?

*W*hen the time is right, mother roo adopts a birthing position that is characteristic of her species. Some sit forward with their tails pointing out between their legs, others lean back against a tree or a rock. Mum then leans down and licks the opening under her tail until a yellow, fluid-filled yolk sac enclosing a minute pink creature appears.

The Big Ascent by Scent

The tiny pink baby breaks free of the yolk sac with its remarkably sharp claws. Guided by its highly sensitive nose, it then commences its momentous ascent up through the thick long fur of its mother's tummy to reach her pouch.

For the duration of the voyage— two to three minutes—the newborn 'swims' up through Mum's fur. To smooth its way, she licks down her fur and occasionally licks the newborn to keep it moist. Fortunately, her fur grows upward. The little one's first voyage is a very long 15–20cm from the birth canal to the warmth and safety of the pouch.

When the baby clambers into the pouch it sniffs its way to one of four teats and latches on. The nipple then swells so that the joey does not slide off.

A typical birthing position but this Whiptail Wallaby already has a pouchful of joey almost ready to pop out its head.

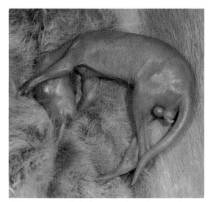

Mission accomplished: teat and newborn make contact. Its hindlegs are completely useless at this stage.

CLUTCHING CLAWS

Like humans' milk teeth, the newborn's sharp little claws that clutch mother's fur on its first day will drop out and be replaced by adult claws.

Can Roos Suspend their Pregnancies?

*R*emarkably, yes. Pregnant kangaroos and wallabies have the ability to put their pregnancy on hold.

At first the mother's fertilised egg divides and multiplies in the normal way but when it grows to a clump of no more than 100 cells, further development may cease if she is already carrying a joey in her pouch or if environmental conditions are poor. For example, drought may trigger her body's pause button. This adaptation is nature's way of cutting down the energy bill. Having babies takes a lot of energy. If

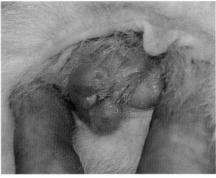

A minute kangaroo foetus latches firmly onto its mother's nipple in the pouch. It is blind, hairless and deaf.

the mother is already feeding and taking care of a joey in the pouch or if food and water supplies are unreliable, her body suspends growth of her foetus until she can provide for it.

How Do Roos Feed Two Babies at a Time?

*I*nside Mum's pouch there are four teats so there's no problem with getting a teat to yourself if you are one of two young ones. The newborn remains tightly

attached to one teat, while an out-of-pouch joey may snack from another.

Joeys of different ages require milk of different compositions. A newborn joey needs low-fat milk, a joey at foot needs high-protein, high-carb milk. How can mum produce both simultaneously? Well, she can and she does. One teat produces low-carb milk for the youngest joey; another produces high-carb milk for the older sibling.

A joey remains dependant on its mother's milk for anywhere from 12 to 18 months, depending on the species.

Although it no longer climbs into Mum's pouch this joey still helps itself to a drink when thirsty.

Why Doesn't Joey Fall Out?

A joey cannot fall out of the pouch unless mother wants it to. The pouch on her belly opens forward and the entrance has a row of muscles that Mum can tighten or loosen at will. The pouch muscles are kept taut until mother decides that the joey is old enough to pop its head out. She then maintains the pouch sufficiently open to afford joey a view but tight enough to prevent him getting out. Finally, when the joey is ready to come out and learn how to jump, she will relax her pouch muscles completely and the joey will literally tumble out onto the ground.

With kangaroos, stomach control takes on new meaning. Without it joey would never survive.

Evicting Joey

The first time Mum lets joey out of the pouch can be a funny scene. This significant event occurs when the young one is between six and 12 months old, depending on the species. The mother will loosen her muscles and joey spills out of the pouch. Because the joey has been supported for all that time, it has no idea how to jump and will stumble or roll around trying to get its balance. The first outing usually doesn't last long as joey is eager to return to the safe refuge of Mum's pouch.

An adult female roo fleeing from danger may save herself by evicting her pouch joey. The short amount of time spent raising that little one is not essential to the survival of the species, but Mum is. Chances are she has a baby on hold ready to climb into the pouch.

> **JELLY BEAN BABY**
> Although perfectly developed, a furless newborn Red Kangaroo is only the size of a baked bean and weighs 1/30,000th as much as its mum.

A newly evicted Bridled Nailtail Wallaby joey looks back longingly into Mum's pouch.

Black-striped Wallaby

The Black-striped Wallaby is listed as common in Queensland but endangered in New South Wales.

Little is known about the Black-striped Wallaby. It is a very shy and increasingly endangered wallaby. Measuring 61–82cm in length, females weigh about 7.5kg, while males can get up to 20kg. The Black-striped Wallaby has grizzled black and brown fur on its face with a white smear on its cheek under and behind its eyes. The torso fur is soft, grey and brown above with light-coloured sides that turn almost white underneath. Its most distinctive marking is the long black stripe running down its back, over its rump and onto its tail, and a white stripe at mid-thigh. The ends of its forepaws, hindlegs, nose and tail are all dark.

The less than graceful movements of the Black-striped Wallaby are distinguished by a short hop, head held low, rump tucked under with forearms stretched out sideways from its stooped body like a hunchback attempting to fly. These wallabies are year-round breeders, with males becoming sexually mature at 20 months and females at 14. They can live for 10 to 20 years.

Shy Yet Social

Populations of Black-striped Wallabies are found all the way from the Townsville region in north Queensland down south to northern New South Wales and throughout much of central Queensland. They live well sheltered on the margins of dense forest or open forests with thick undergrowth, often in brigalow, shrub understorey or vine thicket.

By day groups of up to 20 individuals gather to nibble on grasses and sedges, well concealed from predators, but in areas that have been cleared for crops or pasture these wallabies are known to come out at night to eat. Here they feed on the imported grasses that have supplanted their native food plants. Many farmers consider them pests for this reason and, while cats and foxes are introduced predators that are undoubtedly diminishing their numbers, humans are to be feared just as much.

EXIT ONE BY ONE

When alarmed, Black-striped Wallabies usually move away quickly in single file. Only when there is a major threat do they scatter in all directions.

Red-necked Wallaby

This is a large, attractive wallaby ranging in size from 78cm and 16kg in females to 92cm and 27kg in males. Its body is covered with silver-tipped grey fur and the upper back and shoulders are a rusty red colour. There may be a faded light stripe on the face and/or thigh.

From south-east Queensland, down the New South Wales and Victorian coast and into Tasmania, Red-necked Wallabies are common in the understorey of subtropical and eucalypt forests and woodlands that border open areas. They are even considered a pest by some farmers and plantation growers. In Tasmania, this species is known as Bennett's Wallaby.

The striking contrast between the body and tail colours makes this wallaby particularly attractive. Tasmania's Bennett's Wallaby (right) has thicker fur.

Habits and Breeding

They usually shelter alone in the forest by day and, although mostly solitary, at night they may gather in groups of 30 or more to graze and browse on green shoots to which they are partial in the forest understorey. If alarmed, they hop off in all directions in pairs or singly.

On the mainland Red-necked Wallabies are year-round breeders but in Tasmania they only give birth between February and April. Occasionally these wallabies are commercially harvested.

WALLABIES BRAVE THE ICE AGE
A recent study carried out in Tasmanian caves uncovered a great number of Bennett's Wallaby skeletons. The study revealed that these wallabies were being hunted through the winter months by Aborigines living in caves through the last ice age, 2 million years ago.

Should You Feed Wild Roos?

*F*eeding wild animals is not a good idea because it encourages them to become dependant on humans. If you feed the kangaroos at a campground, for example, the next people who come along will be harassed for food by demanding roos. That's not fair. Kangaroos that are used to being fed by humans can get very aggressive.

Kangaroos and wallabies should never eat processed human foods. White bread is an absolute no-no as it will make them ill and can cause them to lose their fur. Certain zoos and wildlife parks offer specially formulated pellets that the public can feed to the captive kangaroos. These are made with special ingredients that will not harm them.

Kangaroos have specialised diets and should be fed only certain foods.

What Happened to the Toolache Wallaby?

*T*he last recorded sighting of the Toolache Wallaby was in 1939. Once common throughout its restricted south-eastern South Australian range, this graceful animal was hunted almost to extinction for its beautiful fur. Fox predation and the results of land clearing during the late 1800s and early 1900s are credited with the demise of the Toolaches.

Those lucky enough to observe this lovely animal remarked on its speed and agility—particularly noticeable when being chased by dogs. During the early 1920s, several attempts were made to save the species by translocating a few Toolaches to a sanctuary on Kangaroo Island. Unfortunately, these animals died as a result of stress caused by being chased and captured.

> **BULLBARS FOR ROOS**
> An automobile collision with a kangaroo can kill the animal and total the vehicle. Road trains, buses, utes and many cars have a bullbar, or roo bar, mounted on the front to protect the vehicle. Unfortunately it doesn't do much to save the roo.

Highly prized for its beautiful fur, the Toolache Wallaby is now extinct.

Why Are Nailtails So Called?

*S*ticking out from the end of a nailtail's tail is a 'fingernail' 3–6mm long, that looks like half a licorice bullet. Nobody knows what it is for but several interesting theories have recently been proposed.

One theory is that the male drags it behind him drawing squiggles in the sand or dirt as part of his courtship ritual. Another is that he uses it as a balancing tool when travelling at high speed. Still another arises from the fact that nailtails have been observed sitting with their tails in their mouths as if massaging their gums with the tip. Perhaps the nail tip is a tool of dental hygiene, a sort of wallaby's toothpick.

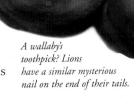

A wallaby's toothpick? Lions have a similar mysterious nail on the end of their tails.

Whatever Happened to the Nailtails?

*T*he Crescent Nailtail's name was inspired by the white crescent behind its forearms. This pretty, hare-sized wallaby once populated large areas of Western Australia, South Australia and the Northern Territory but with European settlement and the clearing of their native habitat, their numbers dived rapidly. In 1927 a Dingo trapper caught a Crescent Nailtail and sent it to the Australia Museum. The last one is variously said to have been killed in the Northern Territory in 1956 (and the wallaby then declared officially extinct), or killed by a fox in 1964.

Bridled Nailtails were almost annihilated through destruction of their habitat by clearing and introduced species. Some farmers considered the Bridled Nailtails pests and put bounties on them. They remain endangered.

The Northern Nailtail is the only species that has continued to thrive.

The once widespread Crescent Nailtail Wallaby became extinct in the 1960s.

Northern Nailtail Wallaby

This sandy-coloured, long-tailed wallaby is the largest of the nailtails and a native of northern Australia. Including their long tail, females are just over a metre long and weigh about 5kg; males may be nearly half as big again and weigh up to 9kg. A dark stripe runs from the lower neck down to the base of the tail, ending in a dark tuft of hair.

The Northern Nailtail Wallaby evolved around two million years ago during the Pleistocene era, when Australia's centre was drying out. Today this arid-country dweller mainly occupies open eucalypt woodlands in the north and shrub savanna in the south.

Some scientists believe that, unlike the Crescent and Bridled Nailtails and the Eastern and Central Hare-wallabies (all now extinct), the Northern Nailtail and the Spectacled Hare-wallaby have survived because the heart of their home range lies north of the country occupied by the rabbit.

The distinctive stripe of the Northern Nailtail finishes in a dark tuft of hair at the end of the tail. This wallaby also has very long, mobile ears.

It prefers herbs over dry grass and will readily consume fruits,

young grass shoots and succulent plants. This solitary nocturnal wallaby feeds from dusk to dawn in groups of no more than four. Shy, flighty and powerful for its size, it can travel at high speed.

When frightened, this wallaby will sometimes freeze, stretch out on its belly or crawl under a bush. It spends most of the day hidden in dense vegetation, lying in shallow scrapes or in hollowed-out tree trunks.

Unlike the Bridled Nailtail, this species has managed to survive quite well despite predatory feral animals and European encroachment on its habitat.

ORGAN GRINDERS

Bridled and Northern Nailtail Wallabies are sometimes called 'organ-grinders' because while hopping they stretch their forearms out in front of them and whirl them in a circular motion.

Western Brush Wallaby

Unusually, male and female Western Brush Wallabies are the same size: about 1.2m long including the tail and 8kg or so in weight. They also look alike, their grey body fur being high-lighted with brown on the head, neck and back. The underside is a dark tan and a white facial stripe runs from mouth to ear. The light-coloured fur on the inside of the ears is rimmed with black. Nicknamed Black-gloved Wallaby, its hands and feet tips are also black, as is the tip of its long tail. Some have faint dark stripes running across their lower back and rump.

A Western Brush Wallaby.

This species lives only in the south-west corner of Australia, in open dry forest, jarrah forest or woodland. A fast mover, it hops low to the ground with its tail extended. Other roos here are nocturnal but this one grazes during early morning and late afternoon on grasses and forbs on wet flats and in open scrubby thickets. Through the heat of the day it rests singly or in pairs.

Listed as threatened, the Western Brush Wallaby was once traded by early settlers and its numbers were further reduced in later years by land clearing and foxes. Today the population appears to be increasing due to fox baiting with fluoroacetate (1080). Births occur mostly during April and May, with joeys leaving the pouch at six months.

Bridled Nailtail Wallaby

This small grey, white and yellowish wallaby measures 83cm to a little over 1m including the tail. Its name comes from the distinctive white stripes with dark borders that start between the ears and run down across the shoulders and under the forearm.

Initially believed to be a solitary animal, recent observations of captive animals have shown that it is in fact very sociable.

In the early 1930s they were believed to be extinct, but in 1973 a small colony was discovered in central Queensland. As a result of breeding and release programs, there are now several growing Bridled Nailtail Wallaby colonies, but their status is still endangered.

On the brink of extinction, this beautiful little wallaby is being successfully bred in captivity.

Do Kangaroos Stress Out?

Kangaroos lick their forearms when they are hot; as the saliva evaporates, the air around it cools. This behaviour may also be a result of stress.

Stress doesn't just kill humans. Roos and wallabies are highly strung animals and severe stress can kill them, too. If a roo is chased, handled badly or captured, it experiences trauma and produces vast quantities of adrenaline which in turn cause a serious condition called 'post-capture myopathy'. This results in muscular dysfunction that is often fatal.

Another stress-related condition is hyperthermia caused by abnormally high body temperatures. If a chased roo begins to lick its forearms to cool itself down, this may be a sign that stress is bringing on hyperthermia. If it sets in, the animal will die.

When is a Red White or Blue?

When it's an albino, or a Blue Flyer. Female Reds are called does and flyers. The ones with grey–blue fur are Blue Flyers.

A white roo in the bush is an easy target for predators. In the wild, albinos are rare. They only occur about once in every 10 000 births. In captivity, however, albinos are much more common because albino parents have a tendency to produce albino offspring.

Albino wallabies are bred as novelty display animals for wildlife parks, where they are a big drawcard for tourists. Generally speaking, albino kangaroos and wallabies are more prone to illness and with each generation the likelihood of poor health increases.

Reds, whites and blues relax together in the sun.

This delicate albino Tammar or Dama Wallaby could easily be mistaken for a giant white rabbit.

What is Fluoroacetate?

*F*luoroacetate, also known as 1080, is a poison widely used around the world to eliminate a variety of pests. In Australia it is used to get rid of foxes, feral dogs and Dingos. It is hoped that by doing this, endangered species will have a better chance of surviving.

Although very effective at decreasing the fox population, 1080 can also be harmful to native Australian mammals.

In Western Australia native animals, such as kangaroos, are immune to 1080 because they eat a native plant from the pea family called *Gastrolobium*. These plants contain the fluoroacetate toxin to which Western Australia's native wildlife has built up a high tolerance. Non-natives, such as rabbits, foxes and domestic stock, however, have not.

It is believed that many native species that have survived the invasion of introduced feral animals and are now in the south-west region of Western Australia were once much more widely distributed throughout the continent. It may well be that the presence of *Gastrolobium* plants in certain regions of Western Australia has helped keep introduced species away, thereby ensuring the survival of native species.

Why Do Some Kangaroos Go Blind?

*I*n the mid-1990s thousands of blind Grey and Red Kangaroos appeared across Australia. Horrible scenes of frightened roos bumping into each other, tripping over bushes and slamming into trees remain a nightmare vividly imprinted in many animal lovers' memories.

The debilitating disease was eventually attributed to two viruses transmitted by midges—tiny biting insects. Scientists believe that the viruses cause retinal damage in macropods only. The viruses have been moving around the northern parts of Australia for thousands of years. Torrential rains throughout the country during the 1990s facilitated the spread of the midges to other parts of Australia. Blind roo numbers have decreased in Western Australia, and they are only occasionally reported in western New South Wales.

Although blind, this doe has raised two joeys successfully—in captivity of course.

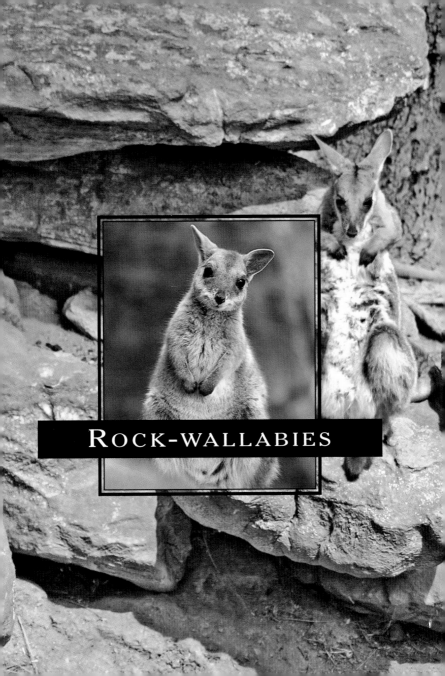

ROCK-WALLABIES

What Is a Rock-wallaby?

*A*s the name suggests, these are wallabies that have adapted to living among rocky outcrops of granite, sandstone or basalt. None are found in Tasmania but many live in rocky ranges throughout mainland Australia. Eleven species of rock-wallabies are found in them there hills.

These agile animals can hop over rocks at mind-boggling speeds despite following irregular paths over uneven surfaces. Like goats, they are incredibly sure-footed.

This Rothschild's Rock-wallaby bounds off rock surfaces like a pingpong ball.

By day rock-wallabies rest in the deep shadows cast by rocks. These provide protection from daytime predators and, in hot climates, shelter from the day's heat. In cool times, they offer protection from the cold and the wallabies come out during warm spells to bask in the sun. They are sociable creatures and often form colonies of up to several hundred individuals.

Rock-wallabies are attractive animals with well-defined markings. When in fast-forward mode they often hold their forearms straight out in front of them. Their tail is long and tube-shaped, not tapered as in other kangaroos and wallabies. It is essentially a balancing tool for safe and effective navigation across the rocks. When the rock-wallaby hops slowly its tail arches over its back for balance but at high speeds it streams straight out behind.

Granite Gorge, a huge granite outcrop on the Atherton Tablelands in northern Queensland is home to this Mareeba Rock-wallaby.

LATCHKEY JOEYS

Unlike other roos and wallabies, the out-of-pouch rock-wallaby joey does not accompany its mother when she forages for food during the day. Rather it stays behind in a chosen shelter with Mum returning periodically for a suckling break.

Hopefully, this sun-bathing Yellow-footed Rock-wallaby joey is on the lookout for predators.

How Do Rock-wallabies Grip Slippery Rocks?

*T*he hindfoot pads of rock-wallabies are reminiscent of the most rugged 4WD tyres. Like specialised rubber wheels, their granulated soles provide a tread that allows them to grip the most slippery rock surfaces. Additional traction is provided by a fringe of tough hairs that grows around the edges of the sole. Rock-wallabies have short toenails on their hindfeet, whereas other kangaroos and wallabies have long toenails. Long nails would get in the rock-wallaby's way, possibly causing it to loose its traction and slip on the rough terrain.

Rock-wallabies have a 'tread' on their feet that helps them grip rocks.

When Is a Rock-wallaby's Home its Prison?

*R*ock-wallabies are believed to have originated in the western part of Australia. Before Europeans arrived, they travelled freely from one rocky outcrop to the next, even if they were many kilometres apart. In those days the terrain in between featured high grasses, dense scrub or trees in which the migrating animals could seek temporary refuge. Today, such migration is impossible due to clearing, the introduction of grazing animals and the arrival of feral predators, such as foxes and dogs. As a result, some rock-wallabies find themselves virtually prisoners on their rocky outcrops.

Trapped in its rocky home, this Mareeba Rock-wallaby is surrounded by hostile agricultural land that would expose him to predators.

BREAKING THE MOULD
The beautiful markings of the rock-wallabies follow the age-old tradition of furry mammals that seek to avoid predators. The patterns of subdued colours help to break up the outline of the animal's body, so a predator has difficulty picking it out against its background.

Black-footed Rock-wallaby

Populations of Black-footed Rock-wallabies are scattered throughout many rocky outcrops of the arid mainland and some western and northern islands of Australia. Once widespread, mainland colonies today have been decimated, particularly by foxes. On islands, where foxes are absent, the wallabies have fared much better.

Standing half a metre tall with a tail another half metre long, and weighing 5–7.7kg this rock-wallaby's thick coat is usually dark brown or grey above and paler underneath. A dark line runs from the centre of its forehead to halfway down its back. Its brown tail usually becomes darker towards its tip.

Reflecting the species' distinctly different locations, there are five subspecies. Among these, coat colours vary and stripes on the face, head and sides, too, are variable.

This rock-wallaby is understandably timid and wary. It tends to stay close to home and only ventures away from its rocky

Only an experienced rock climber could access many ledges occupied by Black-footed Rock-wallabies.

habitat at night to feed on grassy patches nearby. When alarmed it will bolt, doing a pinball impersonation over rocks until it finds a cave or crevice in which to hide.

Mainland Survival in the Balance

Several attempts have been made to manage the Black-footed Rock-wallaby on the mainland but the ongoing battle against introduced species such as rabbits and goats—with which they compete for food—and predators such as foxes and cats, makes the rock-wallaby's long-term survival uncertain. Even the introduction of Buffel Grass, an extremely invasive non-native cattle grass, poses a threat to the Black-footed Rock-wallaby because it takes over the native vegetation, depriving the wallabies of their normal food plants—herbs, native grasses, fruits and low shrubs. The rock-wallabies do, however, thrive on offshore islands and in areas where predators and competitors have been kept under control.

Yellow-footed Rock-wallaby

This rock-wallaby lives in the harsh, dry, rocky regions of central Queensland, South Australia's Flinders Ranges and western New South Wales.

In the 1880s, a naturalist noted that the Yellow-footed Rock-wallaby was 'by far the most abundant of creatures'. However, this colourful ring-tailed wallaby was very popular with the early fur traders and as a result its numbers crashed almost to the point of extinction. Today it is found only in isolated colonies.

The largest of all the rock-wallabies, measuring 1–1.3m including the tail and weighing 6–11kg, the Yellow-footed Rock-wallaby is a browser, preferring shrubs and herbs over grasses. It can jump almost 2m straight up into the air and even further when ricocheting off rock faces.

High Adolescent Mortality Rate

When a joey is finally evicted from the pouch it faces a number of challenges. In addition to its steep rocky habitat, it can fall prey to hungry predators, such as Wedge-tailed Eagles, and is often left on its own—hopefully sufficiently protected among the rocks—when Mum goes off foraging for food.

***

WATER GUZZLERS

After a torrential downpour the Yellow-footed Rock-wallaby has been known to guzzle an astonishing 11% of its own body weight in seven seconds. This feat enables it to survive until the next downpour instead of having to seek out groundwater, which in summer can be hard to find.

***

This young male grooms himself lazily while soaking up some rays.

A vigilant mother sits close to cover, aware of the threat of predators to her joey.

Who's Threatening the Rock-wallabies?

*B*efore Europeans arrived in Australia the rock-wallaby predators were Aborigines, Wedge-tailed Eagles and pythons. The number of animals eaten by these predators was not enough to make a significant dent in their populations. When the Europeans introduced new non-native animals, however, rock-wallabies had new predators and competitors to contend with and in several cases rock-wallaby populations have been all but decimated as a result.

The fox is a fast agile climber, capable of chasing rock-wallabies into their hiding places. Young rock-wallabies left behind in caves or rock shelters by their foraging mothers are particularly susceptible to the prying attention of hungry, wily foxes. Even though goats don't chase and eat rock-wallabies, they do compete for the same type of food and shelter and will readily evict these animals from their homes.

The cunning imported fox is a huge threat to rock-wallaby populations nationwide.

Goats love rocky places and they're eating the rock-wallabies out of house and home.

Who Knows How to Conserve the Northern Rock-dwellers?

*T*oday, many scientific researchers rely increasingly on the invaluable knowledge of the Aboriginal people when undertaking ecological studies in Australia. In order to manage the land and its fauna effectively, it is necessary to incorporate both indigenous and modern scientific knowledge. Aboriginal people have a lot of expert knowledge about the kangaroos and wallabies they have been harvesting sustainably for thousands of years.

What's the Best Bait?

*I*n order to study rock-wallabies scientists trap them. Many traps are made out of hard wire mesh with doors that swing shut when the treadle mechanism is triggered. Rock-wallabies tend to freak out in these traps and bounce repeatedly against the hard mesh in an attempt to escape. This can result in injuries. Some rock-wallabies have figured out how the mechanism works and manage to get at the bait without triggering the door.

The Bromilow Trap

In the late 1980s, Bob Bromilow, an engineer working with Western Australia's Conservation and Land Management (CALM), invented a soft trap, named the Bromilow Trap. This brilliant contraption consists of a metal frame to which strong netting is suspended and attached from the inside. Hessian or shade cloth is wrapped around the outside to make it impossible to get at the tantalising apple

A rock-wallaby unharmed in the soft Bromilow Trap.

pieces without entering the trap. Upon entry, a magnetic latch is triggered that causes the door to slide down and cut off the opening.

When are Rock-wallabies Vitamin C Deficient?

Marsupials make their own vitamin C within their bodies, unlike humans, who have to get it from their diet. The amount of vitamin C they can produce depends on the quality of their food source. The food for rock-wallabies on many islands is not very nutritious, so animals such as the Black-footed Rock-wallaby on the Pearson Islands off South Australia produce only small amounts of vitamin C. As a result, they go berserk when visiting researchers offer them onions, apples and oranges.

Island rock-wallabies just love apples, oranges and onions.

Brush-tailed Rock-wallaby

Teetering on the brink of extinction, a captive breeding program holds hope of recovery for the Brush-tailed Rock-wallaby.

This rock-wallaby is 51–58cm long and its tail is another 50–70cm. It weighs 5–11kg and its fur is thick and bushy. The upper body can be all rufous brown, or the back and shoulders can be grey–brown. The

This rock-wallaby's habitat ranges from rainforest to dry schlerophyll.

lower body is mostly brown and the underside is usually pale. The face has a light cheek stripe and there is a dark black line that runs from behind the eyes down the back of the neck. The long shaggy tail is brown or black. The northern members of this species have shorter and lighter coloured fur.

There are three distinct populations in Australia. The largest is in south-east Queensland. Then there are less than 1000 individuals living in northern New South Wales and a tiny population is hanging on in Victoria where it is the only rock-wallaby species in the State.

This extremely agile rock hopper is mostly active at night when it feeds on grasses and forbs. It spends the cold winter days basking in the sun on warm rocks.

New Zealand Wallabies to the Rescue

In the late 1800s some Brush-tailed Rock-wallabies were transported to New Zealand. Generations on, their relatives have been brought back to Australia to participate in breeding programs that may save the species from extinction. Ironically, they have bred so profusely on the New Zealand island of Kawau that in the eyes of some farmers they are now considered pests.

Rothschild's Rock-wallaby

This golden brown rock-wallaby blends into its background beautifully. One of the largest, it measures 47–60cm in length and its brown or black tail is even longer, about another 55–70cm. Individuals weigh anything from 3.7 to 6.6kg. The ears and the upper part of the head and face are dark brown, switching dramatically to light grey on the bottom half. Rothschild's Rock-wallaby sometimes sports a purplish tinge on the fur of its neck and shoulders, similar to that of Queensland's Purple-necked Rock-wallaby. Although similar to the Black-footed Rock-wallaby, Rothschild's can be distinguished by the lack of a black stripe down its back.

The rock-wallaby's colouring allows it to blend in perfectly with its background.

Chased into Remote and Island Refuges

Yet another victim of the wily fox, Rothschild's Rock-wallaby now lives only in remote areas of central Western Australia among the ironstones of the Hamersley Ranges and on offshore islands in the Dampier Archipelago. Here, these agile rock hoppers shelter among granite outcrops, feeding on the sparse vegetation that dots the harsh terrain.

The survival of this species is largely due to their remote and offshore locations which have remained relatively predator free. Populations of this rock-wallaby used to occur on islands closer to the coast but they were wiped out by foxes and cats that swam over from the mainland to eat them. Mainland colonies are maintained thanks to predator control carried out by park rangers.

Rothschild's was named for Baron Rothschild, the British zoologist and collector who founded London's Rothschild Natural History Museum.

> **PETRIFIED ROCK-ROOS**
> Many rock-wallabies freeze on the spot and stick their forearms out when they are scared.

Can You See the Path?

*B*etween the Rothschild's Rock-wallaby's rocky outcrops there are worn patches of ground. These 'patch paths' lead from one outcrop to another. Instead of a continuous dirt trail worn down by years of hopping, the trail is marked by distinctly smooth spots where stones have been pushed aside and vegetation is unable to grow. Clearly the rock-wallabies are landing directly on the spots, which act like dirt stepping stones through the rocky ground and vegetation. Why take the rough road when you can take the smooth?

Rothschild's 'stepping stones'.

How Do Rock-wallabies Keep Their Cool?

*S*taying cool during hot days in arid regions— where most rock-wallabies live— is part of staying healthy. Rock-wallabies do this by seeking shelter in the cool caves and crevices of their outcrop homes. Studies of some rock-wallaby caves have revealed that when outside temperatures range from 18–46°C the caves remain constant between 27–32°C.

Rock-wallabies must also conserve their bodily fluids in order to survive. Because their habitats have meagre water supplies, they get most of the water they need from their food.

> **SMALL ISLAND ROOS**
> Rothschild's Rock-wallaby is smaller than its mainland counterpart. Maybe island vegetation is less nutritious, or the island animals could belong to a subspecies of the mainland one. Studies of Rothschild's are currently underway to learn about their biology and behaviour.

The best of both worlds: a nice sunny ledge for warming up and a rocky den in which to cool off.

Can You Have a Pet Kangaroo?

*I*n Australia, we are not allowed to keep native animals as pets. Many people believe that kangaroos do not make good pets because they are wild animals. Others think that allowing us to domesticate roos encourages us to appreciate our native wildlife more.

Wildlife carers who hand-raise joeys will admit that it is very hard work. They need to be fed around the clock for a major part of their joeyhood.

Males get testy and territorial when their hormones kick in. Instinctively, roos need to box. This may be cute early on, but it can get painful as they grow to adulthood.

It is not a good idea to have a fully grown kangaroo or wallaby hanging around the house. The space requirements are quite substantial and the average backyard is not likely to be sufficient.

Although cute while young, adolescent male roos can get quite aggressive and territorial…not to mention BIG.

Does Roo Poo Stink?

*B*ecause kangaroos and wallabies are mostly herbivores, their poo, referred to as 'scats' by scientists, does not have the offensive smell that we associate with poo. On the contrary, depending on the species, the scat odour ranges from lightly herbaceous to richly musky. Pademelon and tree-kangaroo scats tend to smell musky as their diets include dark green forest leaves, lush thick grasses and rainforest fruits.

The biggest scats are those of the Red Kangaroo. Red roo poo has a light grassy odour because the roo eats mainly native grasses.

It looks like a rock-wallaby's poo den but it's actually just where gravity has caused many scats to gather.

Mareeba Rock-wallaby

Mareeba Rock-wallabies average 47–49cm tall and weigh 3.8–4.5kg. Their elongated, bear-like faces resemble those of their closest relative, Lumholtz's Tree-kangaroo. They also share their tree-climbing cousin's habit of sitting on their tails and using them for counter-balance, even while in mid-air. The Mareeba's greyish brown fur, with few distinguishing markings, changes shades depending on the rocky habitat it occupies, blending in with limestone, granite or basalt.

Mareeba Rock-wallabies often sit on their tails while grooming themselves.

Only a few thousand Mareeba Rock-wallabies exist today. Colonies are sparsely distributed over a few outcrops scattered around the north-western region of the Atherton Tablelands in Far North Queensland. Populations continue to decrease markedly as farming destroys or fragments their habitats.

How Mareebas Live

The Mareebas are nocturnal marsupials. The rocky outcrops they inhabit provide protection from the elements and predators. In summertime they spend most of the daylight hours in the cool of caves and crevices. When cold, they may sun themselves on rocks close to their shelters in the early morning and late afternoon. Under cover of darkness they leave to graze on newly sprouted grass when available, and herbs and leaves at other times.

Mareeba Rock-wallabies are social animals but males can get very aggressive with one another when it comes to protecting their females, territory and food supplies. Because their territories are so restricted, they fight a lot, resulting in many battle-scarred males.

> **SALTY ROOS**
> Island rock-wallabies live in a very salty environment. On some islands their fur and food get soaked with salt-laden mist and dew. They can't groom as this would mean ingesting huge amounts of salt, so they sunbathe and then shake off the crystals.

Purple-necked Rock-wallaby

Once considered a subspecies of the Black-footed Rock-wallaby, this Purple-necked Rock-wallaby is now officially its own species, *Petrogale purpureicollis*. It measures 49–61cm and weighs 4.7–7kg. Its upper body is primarily grey–brown with light grey shoulders, a red-tinged rump and a brown tail, tipped with black. The characteristic colouring on its head, neck and shoulders may be light pink, bright orange, red or purple and varies in intensity. A brownish stripe goes from between the eyes to the bottom of the neck and a dark patch in the armpit sometimes reaches down to the upper thigh.

This rock-wallaby is primarily a grass eater that lives in rocky regions among hummock grasslands and mulga shrublands in the north-western part of Queensland. Mostly active at night, it rests by day in cool caves and crevices.

The purple pigment, visible here around the neck, is secreted through the skin onto the fur.

Proserpine Rock-wallaby

With a body length of 50–64cm and weighing between 4.2–8.8kg, the endangered Proserpine Wallaby is among the largest of the rock-wallabies. The short upper body fur changes from grey–brown to grey when it is shed in summer. The underside is pale yellow or cream with dark brown armpit patches. A slight purple tinge on the shoulders and stomach has occasionally also been detected on these animals. The grey

This rock-wallaby was named after a Queensland town in and around which it can no longer survive due to feral animals and habitat destruction.

face is long with a thin muzzle and a light stripe that runs from the top of its lip to under its eye. The ears are black inside and brown–orange outside. The tail tends to red at the base turning dark, then black, towards the end, with a white tip.

The home territory of these very shy wallabies is limited to some boulder outcrops in semi-deciduous vine forests and grassy open forests in a tiny area of Queensland's central coast north of Mackay. Here the rock-wallabies venture out during late evening and at night to feed on grasses, forbs and leaves. The distribution of this species is the smallest of all the rock-wallabies.

What Turns a Roo Purple?

*I*n 1924 a Queensland property owner discovered a strange-looking wallaby on his land. The animal's face, neck and head were bright purple. A biologist took it back to Brisbane to study but by the time he arrived, the unusual colouring was gone. For many years, scientists believed that this animal was a subspecies of the Black-footed, Unadorned or even Brush-tailed Rock-wallaby but eventually DNA studies showed it to be a distinct species.

In the 1970s, a study of a small group of captive Purple-necked Rock-wallabies showed that the purple colouration was a water-soluble pigment secreted from glands through the animal's skin, similar to the red cinnabarinic acid found on male and female Red Kangaroos. Colour shades and intensity vary depending on the individual rock-wallaby and on the season. This pigment could act as a scent-marking to attract potential mates, advertise reproductive status or to display dominance. It might also work in some way to deter diseases and parasites.

The challenge now is to find out whether the gland that secretes this colour is found in other animals and if so, what determines the purple colour.

Is the purple pigment a fashion statement, sexual attractant or parasite repellant?

Roos on Holiday Island

*N*umbers of Proserpine Wallabies have suffered a steady decline due to weather changes and the unrelenting encroachment of human development, with its attendant predatory cats and dogs. They dropped so far that in 2000 Queensland Parks and Wildlife put out a warning. Either a new home had to be found for many of these beautiful, shy rock hoppers or the species would become extinct.

The search was on to find a suitable site. It had

Today this endangered Proserpine Rock-wallaby is safe only on islands off the central coast of Queensland.

to be an area that had once figured in the species' historic home range and it had to be predator free. Hayman Island in the Whitsundays fitted the bill nicely. It has boulder outcrops, vine thickets and a bit more rain than neighbouring Gloucester Island, already inhabited by Proserpines.

Wallabies from a captive-breeding program in Townsville were released on Hayman Island in small groups over a period of two years from 1998 to 1999. Although at first quite a few were lost to their natural predators, Wedge-tailed Eagles, numbers appear now to have evened out.

Can Culling Cause Extinctions?

*K*angaroo culling in the 1800s in South Australia was so extreme that, where there used to be thousands of animals roaming the bush around Adelaide, by late that century none were left within hundreds of kilometres of the city.

In 1888 a group of people concerned about roos becoming extinct formed what was probably Australia's first 'green' group: the Flora and Fauna Protection Committee of the Field Naturalists Society of South Australia. Their

Kangaroo culling in the nineteenth century wiped out at least one species of macropod.

primary goal was to stop roo hunting. They petitioned the government and in 1891 it passed an act of parliament protecting kangaroos.

During ensuing years sheep and cattle farmers began to eliminate feral animals and create artificial water supplies. Kangaroos took advantage of both these conditions and multiplied. Some claim that today's population of kangaroos in South Australia is more than double that of humans. South Australian hunters and land clearers did, however, manage to completely wipe out the beautiful but not-so-populous Toolache Wallaby by the middle of the twentieth century.

> **ROO COUNTS**
> Many scientists believe that there are more kangaroos and wallabies in Australia today than when Europeans first settled the continent.

Who Are the North-eastern Rock-Wallabies?

*T*here is an almost continuous row of nine different rock-wallaby species along the east coast of Queensland from Pascoe River on Cape York to the New South Wales border. Only the Proserpine and the Brush-tailed Rock-wallabies stand out as physically different from the other seven. It is almost impossible to

visually tell the difference between the Cape York Rock-wallaby, Godman's, Mareeba, Sharman's, Allied, Unadorned and finally Herbert's Rock-wallaby. They can only be told apart by analysing their chromosmes or by their habitat or geographic location.

There are those who believe that the size of the seven diminishes from south to north and that the three northern species have white-tipped tails but neither of these theories has been confirmed. The colour of fur can vary tremendously within a species, as can distinctive markings.

These rock-wallabies are very special in that their chromosomes are really different and pretty!

This Allied Rock-wallaby lives on Magnetic Island off the coast of Townsville.

What Are Chromosomes?

*C*hromosomes are tiny, threadlike, DNA-containing bodies found in the nucleus of each and every plant and animal cell. They are responsible for transmitting hereditary characteristics—specific features that are passed on from parent plants and animals. Humans have 22 numbered pairs of chromosomes. Kangaroos have between 10 and 24, depending on species.

Genes are pieces of chromosome that influence a particular characteristic such as eye colour in humans, fur colour in animals and leaf shape in plants.

Kangaroos and wallabies display a more extensive range of chromosomal variety than any other marsupial. Sometimes the only way you can tell the difference between Eastern and Western Grey Kangaroos, several types of Black-footed Rock-wallaby and seven species of north-eastern rock-wallabies is by studying their chromosomes. Rock-wallabies carry one of the most diverse arrays of chromosome differences observed in mammals.

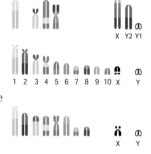

This is the way chromosome pairs are represented diagramatically. The top row shows the genes of the Swamp Wallaby, the middle row the Unadorned Rock-wallaby and the bottom row the Mareeba Rock-wallaby. Compiled by Rachel J. O'Neill, Professor of Genetics, University of Connecticut.

Why Are the Roo and Emu on Australia's Coat of Arms?

*T*he first official coat of arms of the Commonwealth of Australia was granted by King Edward VII in 1908. It showed a shield supported by a kangaroo and an Emu standing on a grassy mound. Above the shield was the crest containing the seven-pointed gold star of Federation on a wreath of white and blue. The motto 'Advance Australia' was inscribed at the base.

Advance Australia

The final and current coat of arms was granted by King George V in 1912. On it is a shield containing the badges of the six Australian States,

Although the emu and the kangaroo are not Australia's official faunal emblems (there are none) they are recognised around the globe as being synonymous with Australia. Permission to reproduce the Commonwealth Coat of Arms granted by the Department of the Prime Minister and Cabinet.

absent on the first coat of arms. The shield continues to be supported by the Red Kangaroo and the Emu. It is said that these two animals were chosen specifically because neither is capable of walking backwards, they can only 'advance' like the new nation of Australia. Four of the eight Australian States and Territories have featured the kangaroo on their coats of arms: Western Australia, Victoria, New South Wales and the Northern Territory.

TOURIST ICON
The results of a recent tourism survey showed that the kangaroo is the second most recognised tourism icon in the world after the Statue of Liberty.

Popular Logo

*K*angaroo and wallaby logos are featured in hundreds of trademarks worldwide. They are used to advertise products as varied as clothing and wine, sports teams and airplanes. Guiness featured the kangaroo in one of its most popular advertisements back in the early 1900s. But probably the best-known kangaroo logo in Australia is Qantas airline's flying kangaroo.

A winning logo for a winning team.

Do Rock-wallabies Inbreed?

*Y*es, unfortunately inbreeding is common. Inbreeding is when members of the same family mate. This results in a loss of genetic diversity which in turn represents a serious threat to the survival of some species.

Inbreeding is the result of habitat fragmentation. Instead of ensuring continuous home ranges for wildlife on their properties, farmers—often

Mareeba Rock-wallabies stranded on rocky outcrop islands frequently end up mating with family members, which weakens their gene pool.

encouraged by government policies—have cleared their land, often leaving only unconquerable rocky outcrop 'islands' where rock-wallaby populations become marooned. With overcrowding and only limited access to food, infighting and inbreeding inevitably occurs.

The daring rock-wallaby who ventures out to found a new colony faces innumerable dangers when it leaves the safety of its rocky home. Foxes, poison baits, motorised vehicles and dogs all threaten its security.

WILDLIFE CORRIDORS

By planting native vegetation across cleared agricultural land wildlife habitats can be linked together to form so-called wildlife corridors. By extending habitat in this way animals can move further afield, thereby reducing population pressure and the likelihood of in-breeding.

Do Rock-wallabies Interbreed?

*I*nterbreeding is when members of different species mate and produce a hybrid, an offspring from parents that are genetically different, like a mule, the offspring of a male donkey and a female horse. The offspring of both interbreeding and especially inbreeding (above) can be genetically weak and prone to health problems.

Near a small town north-west of Brisbane the Herbert's Rock-wallaby is known to interbreed with the Brush-tailed Rock-wallaby and produce a hybrid.

Hybrids are rarely produced in the wild but they do occur in captivity. Female Eastern Greys in captivity have produced hybrids with male Western Greys but female Western Greys will not produce hybrids with male Eastern Greys.

This hybrid is the unhealthy product of a mating between an Agile Wallaby and a larger kangaroo.

Who Are Rock-wallabies' Greatest Predators?

*T*he traditional enemies of the rock-wallabies have been Wedge-tailed Eagles. Soaring high above their rocky homes, eagles can spot the wallabies easily enough once they venture out from the deep shadows of gorges and caves. Wedgies still remain a major concern for rock-wallabies but a number of other predators introduced by humans have multiplied the list of animals to watch out for.

Their eyes may be bigger than their stomachs but this python won't have to eat again for several months now.

First came the Dingos. Dingos have been on the Australian continent for 3000–4000 years and have found wallabies much to their taste, when they can catch them. Dingos usually stick to joeys but they will attack big old male roos if they are in a weakened state. The cunning fox is another serious worry for rock-wallabies. Small enough to sneak into small hiding places and with an excellent sense of smell, it has greatly contributed to the depletion of rock-wallaby populations in many places. For the plains kangaroos and wallabies, dogs, working in packs, are a serious threat.

Small wallabies are also relished by some Australian pythons. One meal goes a long way.

Why Does Joey Lick Mother's Lips?

*J*oeys often lick their mothers' lips for several minutes at a time. It is believed that this is not merely an act of bonding. It may well be a way of passing on vital digestive micro-organisms from the mother kangaroo to her young. Licking Mum's lips can also provide a drink for young joeys when both water and Mum's milk are scarce.

No, they're not just kissing. Joey's taking his medicine.

Monjon

This, the smallest of all the wal-labies, measures only 30–35cm and weighs less than 1.5kg—even a mature male. 'Monjon' is an Aboriginal word for 'very small rock-wallaby'. Another common name is 'Warabi'. The Monjon's olive-coloured back is marbled with black and fawn. Its flanks are a deep olive and the underside yellowish. The tail, which is an olivey grey at its base becomes bushy and dark towards the end. It has an orange face with a light stripe that runs from eye to ear.

Almost 50 times smaller than the big Red Kangaroo, the little Monjon is the tiniest kangaroo species.

This mostly nocturnal wallaby lives in the remote sandstone country of the Kimberley where it spends the day at rest in crevices. At night it feeds on grasses and ferns in the tropical and sub-tropical woodlands. It is also found on the Mitchell Plateau and Bigge Island. Mitchell Falls is one of the more accessible places to view these animals. The Monjon breeds year-round.

Short-eared Rock-wallaby

The Short-eared Rock-wallaby is less than a metre long, including its long bushy tail. Its fur is light grey to brown above and paler underneath. Although we know it lives among rocky outcrops, gorges and cliffs near savanna, forests and woodlands, its inaccessi-bility has made it very difficult to study and we have much to learn about it.

Short-eared Rock-wallabies only occur in northern Australia. They are inhabitants

Aboriginal people of northern Australia are careful not to overhunt Short-eared Rock-wallabies.

of the Kimberley, Arnhem Land and the western part of the Gulf of Carpenteria. As well as Wedge-tailed Eagles and the usual introduced suspects that plague the lives of rock-wallabies—except foxes, which haven't yet made it that far north—the local Oenpelli Python hunts among the rocks for this wallaby.

Nabarlek

This small grey to light brown bushy-tailed rock-wallaby weighs, at the most, 1.6kg and measures no more than a metre from head to tail tip. Until the recent discovery of the Monjon, it was believed to be the smallest of all the macropods.

Strangely enough, this little guy's name is more often than not pronounced 'nar-bah-lek'.

Nabarlek populations are scattered throughout the rocky regions of the Kimberley and parts of the Top End. Their range overlaps that of the Short-eared Rock-wallabies and the Monjons but they do not interbreed with either species, despite their close resemblance to the Short-eareds. The Bininj Aboriginal people who inhabit the region can distinguish these species by their markings and the length of their foreheads. A telltale sign, however, is how the Narbarlek curls its tail over its back when jumping.

Teeth to Take On a Tough Diet

For choice the Narbarlek prefers to eat grass but this is only available during the wet season. In the dry season, with few grasses available, it often eats a particular fern that contains up to 26% silica. This highly corrosive substance is usually enough to discourage animals from eating it but the Nabarlek appears undaunted, perhaps because it has a clever adaptation unknown in any other kangaroo or wallaby. Although its teeth are continuously being worn down, it is capable of producing a limitless number of replacement teeth throughout its life.

■ *Nabarlek*
□ *Short-eared*
■ *Overlap*

Why Are Kangaroo Roadkills So Common?

A sad and all too frequent sight on our rural roads.

*K*angaroos and wallabies are mostly out and about from late afternoon to early morning. If an animal's home range is anywhere near a road, chances are, sooner or later, it will want to cross it. Blinded by the headlights of passing cars or trucks, animals tend to freeze and get hit, often fatally.

During the dry season in the north or during droughts roadkills become especially common because condensation from the exhaust of passing traffic 'waters' the roadside grass, drawing starving roos to the irresistible green pickings.

What Do You Do If You Hit a Roo?

A dead kangaroo lying in the middle of the road can be a traffic hazard. It also attracts other native wildlife, such as Wedge-tailed Eagles, crows, buzzards and kites. Considerate drivers will drag the carcass to the side of the road to reduce the risk of another accident and to prevent further wildlife from getting killed.

Over 10 000 insurance claims are made yearly for kangaroo-related vehicle accidents.

If the dead roo is a female, check the pouch. If there is a pinky (hairless joey) attached to the teat the suction will be so strong that you may injure the baby if you try to pull it off. Place your finger between the joey's mouth and the mother's teat to release enough pressure to remove the little one. Keep it warm. Wrap it in a soft cloth and stick it down your shirt front to keep it cosy. Locate a wildlife carer by looking in the phone book or ringing the nearest parks and wildlife office. A bigger, furred joey can be removed and put in a temporary pouch such as a pillow case or a T-shirt with one end tied to form a bag. Get it to the nearest vet or wildlife carer as soon as possible.

> **HOW TO AVOID HITTING ROOS**
> The surest way to avoid a collision with a kangaroo is not to drive at night. If you must drive, do so slowly, use your high beams and stay alert.

What Do We Do with Orphaned Joeys?

A female kangaroo hit by a car may have a joey in her pouch. There may also be an out-of-pouch joey hiding nearby. Unless rescued, the young will die of starvation. Many wildlife carers in Australia carry a pillow case in their cars that can form a temporary pouch while a joey is transported.

If an orphan is lucky enough to be rescued and handed over to an experienced wildlife carer, it may survive. The older the joey, the better chance it

Keeping a pinky warm is vital to its survival.

has. Pinkies under 500g are very much at risk, whereas joeys that have at least started to grow fur and have open eyes are more likely to survive. Orphans quickly transfer their loyalties to their new mother.

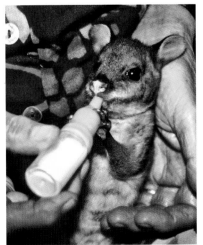

Raising an orphaned joey is a full-time job. Pouch young must be fed at least every two hours around the clock.

Substitute Pouches

To make sure that the little roo is warm enough, carers often carry it around in a pouch down their shirt front so it can benefit from human body heat. An insulated home-made 'pouch' or pillow case hung from a coat hanger or the back of a chair close to, but off, the ground is the most common way of keeping orphaned roos.

Special Formula Milk

Dairy milk will make orphaned pouch joeys very sick. They must be fed a milk formula that is akin to their mother's milk. It is important that carers know exactly what they are doing. Formulae vary with age. There are several commercial ones available through vets and carer organisations.

Once ready to emerge from the artificial pouch, the joey is encouraged to nibble grass and other plants specific to its species. Human food is not recommended, although the occasional slice of sweet potato is a greatly appreciated and harmless treat.

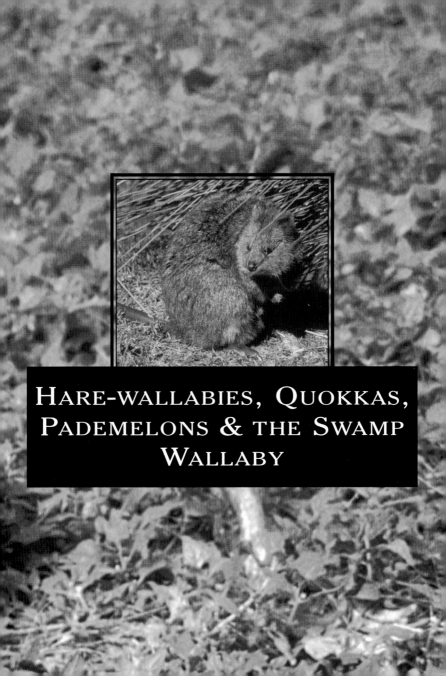

HARE-WALLABIES, QUOKKAS, PADEMELONS & THE SWAMP WALLABY

Why Burn in Patches?

*F*or thousands of years, Aborigines carefully burned specific patches of land in order to encourage new growth of tender grasses, shrubs and bushes— food for their game animals, including kangaroos and wallabies. The burning also served as insurance against devastating wildfires. Because the land was burned in small patches only, there were always other patches available for the wildlife to feed and shelter in while the burned ones regenerated. This is an

excellent means of conserving wildlife and enhancing their habitat. Today this prehistoric practice is being revived and is carried out by parks and wildlife professionals worldwide.

Joseph Lycett's 1830 painting shows Aborigines burning off the bush, driving roos out into the open.

Do Kangaroos Eat Meat?

*A*lthough primarily herbivorous, kangaroos are known to indulge in carnivorous behaviour. Insects are frequent items on the macropod menu. Hand-raised macropods, such as tree-kangaroos and wallabies, will wolf down a piece of cooked chook with great gusto. Kangaroos that inhabit coastal areas where the vegetation is particularly nutritionally poor will not hesitate to eat seaweed or fish and Grey Kangaroos have been observed gnawing dried mammal bones, especially after periods of drought.

We have yet to establish whether eating meat other than insects is a standard part of any macropod's diet or whether it is consumed simply to fill a nutritional void.

This Western Grey is thoroughly enjoying a herring that has been washed up on the beach.

Who Are the Hare-wallabies?

*T*he hare-wallabies were so named because of their resemblance to the European hare. When the Europeans first settled in Australia over 200 years ago, there were five species of hare-wallaby. Today, the Central and Eastern Hare-wallabies are extinct, the Rufous and Banded Hare-wallabies are rare and the Spectacled Hare-wallaby numbers are diminishing. The Rufous and the Banded Hare-wallabies have lived together for over 8000 years on north-western Australian islands that were cut off from the mainland by the rising seas.

The Odd One Out

The Banded Hare-wallaby isn't really a 'hare-wallaby' at all and is only a very distant relation to the other four hare-wallabies. It is, in fact, the sole survivor of a large group of short-faced kangaroos that existed thousands of years ago. They were called the sthenurines.

Intruders, mates and food all have smells. This Spectacled Hare-wallaby sniffs the air to pick up information about its surroundings.

ABORIGINAL NAMES
The Rufous Hare-wallaby is commonly called by its Aboriginal name, Mala. Believe it or not there are over 30 other Aboriginal names for this species: Witjari, Wurrup, Parranti and Matjirri are just a few.

These two Rufous Hare-wallabies at Alice Springs Desert Park are part of a captive breeding program that may assist their long-term survival.

A carnivorous kangaroo attacking a short-faced sthenurine—a very possible scenario 5 million years ago.

Rufous Hare-wallaby or Mala

The thick shaggy fur of the Rufous Hare-wallaby is tinged with red. The back and tail are dappled with silvery grey and the forearms and underarms are a light tan. The muzzle has a white milk-moustache and the outer edges of the large, rounded ears are also white. This delicate little wallaby is more commonly known as the Mala. The female measures no more than 31cm and weighs about 800g, whereas the male reaches 39cm in length and weighs up to 2kg.

Malas blend in well with the red dirt and spinifex hummocks where they shelter and feed on grasses, herbs, seeds and insects.

Rufous Hare-wallabies live among the hummocks of spinifex grasslands and sandy deserts. They used to be widespread throughout the central deserts but as the south temperate grasslands gave way to the wheatbelt, and woodlands were cleared, the mainland Rufous Hare-wallabies disappeared. They are now one of the most endangered species in the world and recently in the Northern Territory they have been declared 'extinct in the wild'.

The animals from a successful captive breeding colony set up in the Tanami Desert have been transferred to Watarrka, south-west of Alice Springs but attempts to release these little hoppers have failed because there are too many predators in their release sites. However, Conservation and Land Management (CALM) in Western Australia is presently running a successful breeding and reintroduction program called Western Shield in the Dryandra woodlands. Although this is a large area, it has been made predator-proof, so technically speaking the Malas are still not living absolutely wild.

Life in the Wild

The only Rufous Hare-wallabies known to be still living completely wild are found on islands. They are considered to be a different subspecies to the mainland animals. They live on Dorre and Bernier Islands off the coast of northern Western Australia and the mainland form has been introduced to Trimouille Island off the Pilbara coast of Western Australia. In total around 4000 individuals are estimated to be still living wild.

DIGGER ROOS
Malas are diggers and shelter in scrapes under scrub. The island ones, having nothing to fear, excavate single-entrance burrows that are poorly concealed.

Spectacled Hare-wallaby

This enchanting little wallaby measures 48–52cm in body length, with a tail almost as long, and weighs 1.6–4.5kg. It has earned its name from the orange patch of fur surrounding both eyes, giving it the appearance of a hopping bandit. It is a thick chubby wallaby with a short wide muzzle sporting a white moustache and beard. The slightly pointed ears are orange at the base and trimmed with white fur. The body is grey–brown, speckled with golden highlights, and the underside is pale.

This delightful spectacled macropod is a camouflage expert.

Keeping a Low Profile

This creature is a master of camouflage and you are likely to trip over one before you become aware of its presence. When frightened it tends to scrunch as far down as it can in the hope of melting into the background. If it does run in the face of danger, it bolts at high speed and can jump over 2m high. A solitary animal, it is rarely seen in groups of more than three and then only while feeding.

Curiously, this animal has never been observed drinking water either in the wild or in captivity, not even opportunistically. Chances are it obtains what it needs from its food, which consists primarily of spinifex, preferably the tips of the leaves. Because it consumes little or no water, it pees very little as well, much less than any other animal of the same size.

Shrinking Habitat

Prior to the arrival of Europeans, the Spectacled Hare-wallaby inhabited almost the entire northern half of Australia. Today its distribution is very patchy and its numbers greatly reduced. Although abundant on Barrow Island off Western Australia, only a few individuals have been spotted in recent years on Western Australia's mainland. In the Northern Territory, too, its range has been significantly constricted. In Queensland the numbers are comparatively high although, due to widespread clearing and development, an estimated 20–30% of their habitat has been destroyed.

What's Being Done for the Mala?

*A*s a result of hard work and cooperation between scientists, researchers, Northern Territory and Western Australian conservation agencies and the Aboriginal Warlpiri people, two groups of captively bred Rufous Hare-wallabies are now living safely in a 20-hectare predator-controlled Western Australian conservation reserve at Dryandra.

This Mala inspects a bug presumably with a view to eating it.

> **ELIXIR FOR THE AGED**
> Aborigines cooked the Mala's blood in the body cavity and used it as medicine for the elderly.

There are also more than 200 Mala in a 100-hectare predator-controlled area at Watarrka. Plans are also underway to construct predator-controlled areas at Uluru (Kata Tjuta National Park) and at Scotia Sanctuary in western New South Wales.

How the Hare-wallaby Found a Home

*I*n 1907 a hospital for Aboriginal men was opened on Dorre Island. The women went to another hospital on Bernier Island nearby. Patients were encouraged to live as traditionally as possible and hunting the local hare-wallabies had always been a favourite activity. The patients remained on the islands for ten years. When they left, the hare-wallabies were still there.

In 1957 the islands were gazetted as reserves for the preservation of wildlife, allowing the hare-wallabies to live in peace.

Today these World Heritage-listed islands are home to five threatened mammal species including the Banded Hare-wallaby and the Rufous Hare-wallaby.

A pouched Banded Hare-wallaby learns how to eat by mimicking Mum.

Can You Mix Genes?

Yes, you can cross-breed an island and a mainland Quokka, or a Kangaroo Island Wallaroo and a mainland wallaroo but many scientists believe that it is not a good idea. They think that the island Quokkas, for example, no longer have an ideal gene pool on offer because they have been restricted to Rottnest Island for ten thousand years, thereby almost assuredly in-breeding. The mainland variety is more likely to have a healthier gene pool. Bringing mainland Quokkas to the island would be more beneficial.

Scientists are worried that inbred Rottnest Island Quokkas have a weak gene pool.

Where's Wallie?

Kangaroos are masters of camouflage. There might be dozens of large roos lying in a field next to a road during the day but unless one of them moves, or you are looking very carefully, you will not see them. Red kangaroos tend to blend in with the red earth of their outback habitat. Greys disappear against the colours of the plains and wallaroos are difficult to distinguish from the rocks amongst which they live.

Rock-wallabies blend in with their rocky backgrounds. Although up close their fur appears colourful and has interesting patterns, against the rocks they are nearly invisible. Spectacled Hare-wallabies disappear into tufts of spinifex and Agile Wallabies melt into high grasses. No matter what shape or size kangaroos are, every species has the ability to blend into its background, thereby giving it a better chance of survival.

A Spectacled Hare-wallaby peeps out from his well-camouflaged hideout.

Banded Hare-wallaby

The Banded Hare-wallaby is the sole survivor of a prehistoric group of flat-faced kangaroos, the sthenurines. Its face is still short and it has small, rounded ears. It stands only about 40–45cm high and its tail is almost as long again. Animals do not exceed 2kg in weight. Their long, thick fur is grizzled grey with golden or silvery overtones above and reddish tints on the lower sides. The Banded's distinguishing marks are the horizontal dark bars that run across its lower back and tail base.

The Banded Hare-wallaby is a nocturnal browser that eats low shrubs and spinifex. Like the Quokka, it spends much of its time on all fours. Small groups of these social animals share mealtimes, nesting sites in thickets or under thick brush, and shelter under low bushes.

The male of this species is very aggressive when competing for food with other males but rarely does he turn against females.

The characteristic dark bands of fur on this wallaby's body are unlike any other patterns found on kangaroo fur.

An Islander

Prior to the 1900s this wallaby ranged across the eucalypt woodlands of south-western Australia as well as inhabiting islands off the central west coast but hunting, land clearing and feral animals totally wiped out mainland populations. Today wild members of the species are found only on Dorre and Bernier Islands off the coast of northern Western Australia. Banded Hare-wallabies have recently been introduced onto nearby Faure Island. The Department of Conservation and Land Management (CALM) staff at the Peron Captive Breeding Centre in Denham, Western Australia, have successfully bred these delightful creatures for release on Peron Peninsula and islands in the Shark Bay area. A survey undertaken in 1989 estimated that their numbers were around 7000.

> **PROTECTIVE MUMS**
> Early explorers were impressed by how protective Banded Hare-wallaby mothers were of their offspring. Even when being hunted, wounded mothers valiantly tried to keep their young from being caught or kicked them out of the pouch and encouraged them to run for safety.

Quokka

Unlike most other kangaroos and wallabies, Quokkas can walk on all four limbs.

Early explorers mistook the Quokka for a large rat and named their island Rottnest, Dutch for 'rat's nest'.

The Quokka is a small wallaby less than a half metre long and weighing around 3kg. Its rounded body is covered with long, thick, coarse grey–brown fur. It has a small head, with a flat face, a long pointed snout and small, rounded ears. The tail is short—a mere 28cm—and almost hairless. The small, hairy paws at the end of its short forearms have sharp claws. Not only can it hop, it can also walk on all fours, which is unusual for members of the kangaroo family.

Island and Mainland Quokkas

Once very common on the mainland in southern Western Australia, Quokkas lived in moist areas with thick, low vegetation, like swamps, and beside streams. Before Europeans settled in Western Australia, Quokka was a frequent item on the Aboriginal people's menu. With the Europeans came foxes, dogs and cats, which caused massive declines in mainland Quokka numbers. In the 1960s only a very few remained in Perth swamps. More recently, thanks to fox baiting, the numbers there have increased.

> **QUOKKA MALES RULE**
> In Quokka society, the older the male, the more authority he has over younger males, females and their joeys. The same goes for the majority of roo species.

Today Quokkas—approximately 10 000 of them—are mostly restricted to Rottnest Island where the low and scrubby coastal vegetation is nutritionally poor and fresh water is scarce, coming primarily from seeps. The remaining mainland Quokkas live in isolated swampy thickets along the southern coast.

What Were Prehistoric Roos Like?

*I*t would seem that the first kangaroos evolved from tree-dwelling creatures that descended to the ground in their search for food. The earliest kangaroo-like animals that have so far been found in the fossil record were small roos that walked on all fours. They lived in cool dry forests and ate soft plants. They had sharp buck teeth, strong arms and relatively small hindlegs on which they did not hop.

Between 23 and 6 million years ago there were lots of different species of kangaroos; in fact there were more than there are today. Many were carnivorous and lived in rainforests. Scientists believe that carnivorous kangaroos were still around when the first humans arrived in Australia maybe 50 000 years ago. One such was the ferocious strong-clawed, sharp-toothed killer kangaroo *Ekaltadeta ima*,

Some prehistoric kangaroos, both large and small, were fierce, sharp-toothed meat-eaters.

whose bones were discovered at Riversleigh, near Mt Isa in Queensland.

When Kangaroos Began to Hop

Somewhere between 15 and 6 million years ago, hopping, leaf-eating roos appeared in open woodlands. Only in the last 2 million years have the familiar large, grass-eating roos been hopping across the land in any great numbers.

Around 200 000 to 50 000 years ago a large, short-faced kangaroo called *Simosthenurus occidentalis* appeared in the open forests. Its hindlegs had a single toe that resembled a horse's hoof, which suggests it was probably adapted to moving over level ground. It was the same size as today's Grey Kangaroo but much stouter. In Latin *simo* means short-faced and *sthenurus* means strong tail. It browsed on shrubs and small bushes and could reach leaves high above the ground with its long forearms. Its large, wombat-like jaw and sharp teeth suggest that it was able to eat tough plants. Today, the only remaining direct descendant from this line of kangaroos is the Banded Hare-wallaby.

How Do Quokkas Cope with Drought?

*O*n the arid islands inhabited by some wallabies there is no fresh water for much of the year. Although Quokkas on Rottnest Island can do without water for months at a time, they lose weight and become anaemic under these conditions and sometimes they die. It is probably the lack of fresh water on the islands that accounts for why island animals only breed from January to March, while mainland Quokkas breed all year round.

Quokka breeding seasons may be reduced by irregular access to fresh water.

What's a Pademelon?

*T*hey are little wallabies about a metre in length, including their tails. The three species in Australia are: the Red-legged, the Red-necked and the Tasmanian (otherwise known as the Red-bellied Pademelon). Their coats come in reds, greys and browns, not specific to species. Short and stocky, they hunch forward when standing and stay close to the ground when darting forward.

Pademelons are found as far north as the tip of Cape York and as far south as Tasmania. Their preference is for moist habitats with ready access to green grass. They mostly inhabit rainforests that border open areas. Unlike some kangaroos, they are very clever with their little paws and and are able to manipulate food quite well.

A Red-necked Pademelon takes time out to scratch.

Red-legged Pademelon

This is the smallest of the three pademelons. Excluding their 30cm-long tails, females are about 39cm tall and weigh about 4.2kg. Males are maybe 54cm tall and weigh about 6.5kg. The fur is short but thick: red on the face, sides and hindlegs and speckled grey–brown on its back, neck and shoulders. There is a white stripe on the cheek and a dark line from mid-forehead to the top of the head.

The Red-legged Pademelon is primarily a browser but will happily crop grass, too.

The Red-legged Pademelon is one of only two Australian macropods that are also found in New Guinea (the other being the Agile Wallaby). Its Australian populations stretch from Queensland's Cape York all the way down to the north coast of New South Wales where this species' range overlaps with that of the Red-necked Pademelon. Red-legged Pademelons are inhabitants of rainforests, wet eucalypt forests and vine scrubs.

Group Feeders Employ Sentries

Red-legged Pademelons mainly browse but late in the day, at night and early in the morning they can be found nibbling on grass in clearings at the edge of the forest. Their favourite food includes ferns, leaves that fall off tall rainforest trees and fruits. Groups of other species of pademelons tend to scatter at the first sign of danger but the Red-leggeds often stick together, relying on sentries to alert them to any impending danger by thumping their feet on the ground. Amethystine Pythons, humans, Tiger Quolls and Dingos are their commonest predators. Seldom do they venture more than 100 metres from the forest's edge. Creatures of habit, they follow well-worn runways and tunnels through the vegetation to and from their rainforest refuges.

Red-necked Pademelon

Except for the pale underside, the colouring of the Red-necked Pademelon is almost the reverse of that of the Red-legged—shoulders, neck and forehead are a rich red and the upper body is a speckled grey–brown. The tail is short and thick. Females average 32cm in length and 4kg in weight, while males are closer to 60cm and 7kg.

Rainforest Refuges Always Close at Hand

Dwellers of the rainforests and wet sclerophyll forests along the coast of south Queensland and northern New South Wales, these pademelons will roam around the rainforest during the day and emerge out onto fields at night to graze on grasses, forbs and small

Red-necked Pademelon, with the typical red on the shoulders and neck.

shrubs. At the first sign of danger, Red-necked Pademelons dash into the dense rainforest for refuge, where their customary predators—Dingos, owls, Wedge-tailed eagles and foxes—may find it hard to follow. Like their cousins, these pademelons hop along well-worn pathways. Although Red-necked Pademelon numbers are still relatively high, continuous and persistent land clearing is bound to pose a threat to their population in the future.

Tasmanian Pademelon

Also known as the Red-bellied Pademelon, this squat little wallaby has very thick fur to keep it warm during the freezing winter nights. On its back the fur is dark brown, tan and grey and underneath a reddish tan. Around the eyes and at the base of the ears there is a reddish tint, while the areas around the mouth and under the muzzle are tan. Females stand 55cm tall and can weigh almost 6kg, while males may be 63cm tall and weight up to 9kg. The short, thick tail is only two-thirds of the body length.

The Tasmanian Pademelon is a solitary animal that spends most of its daylight hours in dense vegetation bordering cleared areas into which it will venture (never more than 100m) to feed at night. Its habitat is rainforest, wet forests and occasionally wet gullies in euca-

Previously found on the southern mainland, today's Tasmanian Pademelon population is restricted only to the island State.

lypt forests. It relies on the dexterity of its forelimbs to uncover food, especially when it has to dig in the snow to eat during the wintertime. Its favourite meal is short green grass but it will eat herbs, green shoots and sometimes even nectar-filled flowers and moss.

Quick to React to Danger

Although it will feed in groups, this pademelon scatters when alarmed. When in a hurry it hunches down with its head low, its back flat and the tail stuck straight out behind as it shoots forward so fast you wonder if it has actually touched the ground.

> ### NOT ALWAYS A TASWEGIAN
> The Tasmanian Pademelon once lived in the southern parts of Victoria and South Australia but it quickly became extinct upon arrival of the Europeans. It remains common on the island State.

The Tasmanian Pademelon used to be a favourite on the menu of the now extinct Tasmanian Tiger. Its pelt was once highly prized among fur traders. Today, predators include the Tasmanian Devil, human beings and the Spotted-tailed Quoll. It is also considered a pest by farmers and plantation owners and is still culled on a regular basis.

Most Tasmanian Pademelon births take place at the onset of winter. Their lifespan does not usually exceed five or six years in the wild.

Swamp Wallaby

Swamp Wallabies are browsers and their diet is one of the most diverse of all the kangaroos.

Because the genetic make-up of the Swamp Wallaby is so different from that of other wallabies, it is in a class of its own. It is also unique in another way: instead of waiting for joeys to be born prior to conceiving another—as other wallabies do—female Swamp Wallabies will mate right up to eight days before giving birth.

Quite a chunky wallaby, females weigh up to 15kg and grow to 75cm. Males weigh up to 20kg and can stand up to 85cm tall. A Swamp Wallaby's tail is as long as its body and, in the case of males, it is white-tipped. The face is dark with pale markings on the cheek. The fur is dark, coarse and thick, primarily shiny dark grey or black on top with gold or red highlights turning to pale yellow or reddish orange on the underside. Northern species are reported to be redder.

The Swamp Wallaby is a hardy survivor. From the tip of Cape York to south western Victoria it prefers living in wet or dry sclerophyll forests but it is also found in mangroves, rainforests, heathland and woodland where it takes cover in the understorey grasses.

An Adaptable Eater

From the study of its teeth it is believed that the Swampy went from an open grassy woodland grazer, like the Red and Grey Kangaroos, to eating soft herbage. Surprisingly, clover and grasses, the preferred food of most of the larger kangaroos, are not the Swampy's first choices. It would rather munch on gum leaves, dogwoods, sedges, rushes, pine tree seedlings, fungi and even poisonous introduced hemlock and Bracken Fern. It is a solitary browser with an amazing ability to adapt to a wide variety of diets. In captivity it has been known to wolf down anything on offer, including meat, cheese and bikkies.

> **FEWER CHROMOSOMES**
> Most wallabies have 16 chromosomes. The male Swampy has 11, the female only 10.

TREE-KANGAROOS

What Is a Tree-kangaroo?

*Y*es, you've guessed it. It's a kangaroo that spends over 90% of its life in tree-tops. Here it eats, sleeps, breeds, plays and raises its young.

There are twelve existing tree-kangaroo species. Ten reside in New Guinea and east Indonesian neighbouring islands, and two are found in Far North Queensland: the Lumholtz's and the Bennett's Tree-kangaroos.

The Lumholtz's is the smallest of all the tree-roos and the Bennett's is only slightly larger. In both species the males are solitary but females remain in small family groups composed of a few adults, some out-of-pouch joeys and some in-pouch joeys.

Bennett's Tree Kangaroo is the larger of the two Australian tree-roo species.

Studies show that both Australian tree-kangaroos are very territorial. The territories of males overlap those of 'their' females but never those of other males. Females' home ranges can overlap as well.

Where's Joey?

*T*he period of pregnancy of a tree-kangaroo is longer than any other kangaroo or wallaby: 45 days. Whereas most mothers keep their young nearby for eight months to one year, a Lumholtz's Tree-kangaroo joey stays with its Mum for at least two years, even longer if it is female.

The Lumholtz's Tree-kangaroo joey stays in the pouch for 10 to 12 months, then remains close by for at least another two years. This

This inquisitive young Lumholtz's is a bundle of energy, quite a handful for Mum to keep track of.

may be because it takes the mother that long to teach her offspring all it needs to know to survive in the rainforest on its own. For example, it needs to be able to tell the difference between edible and toxic leaves.

While her young charge hops from branch to branch, climbs up and down trunks and walks—yes, Lumholtz's Tree-kangaroos actually puts one hindfoot in front of the other—Mum may sit aloof and sedate perched high up on rainforest branches. To watch this agile, ambulatory kangaroo is delightful and enough to melt the hardest heart.

Who Was Lumholtz's Tree-roo Named After?

*W*hen Norwegian explorer Carl Lumholtz, a theologian turned biologist, was told by local indigenous people in 1882 about a dog-sized tree-dwelling kangaroo that they called 'boongar', he was determined to see one for himself. His relentless pursuit of the have-to-see-it-to-believe-it creature eventually won him the honour of having the species named after him.

Lumholtz's Tree-kangaroo is virtually undetectable in the forest canopy.

What's a Tail Good For?

*T*he tree-kangaroo's impossibly long tail—sometimes more than three quarters of a metre—hangs down from the branch upon which it sits. This extremity, long and thick with the last third bushier and darker than the rest, serves as a balancing and propping appendage. The roo uses it to balance its body when clambering about in the trees but the tail cannot grip things like some monkeys' tails do. It is often sat upon while the tree-roo naps with its head tucked into its lap. This habit is shared by some of the tree-roos' distant relatives—the Mareeba, Proserpine and Allied Rock-wallabies.

> **WHO ELSE CLIMBS TREES?**
> The Proserpine Wallaby, and both the Mareeba and Unadorned Rock-wallabies, have also been observed climbing trees.

The tree-roo's tail is not prehensile and cannot wrap around things. It is merely a balancing tool and prop.

Lumholtz's Tree-kangaroo

Lumholtz's Tree-kangaroo has a black elongated bear-like face framed by a yellowish grey chin-band that extends up its cheeks and down its throat to its chest. From above, the body of this squat, furry kangaroo is dark grey to black; the underside is pale and the front and back feet are black, as is the end of its bushy tail. The front legs are strong and muscular, designed for the strenuous work of climbing. Among sexually mature males an orange-coloured pigmentation on the inner thigh is apparent. Lumholtz's weighs 5–11kg and its body measures 52–65cm with a tail well over half this length again. The female is smaller.

Life on the Tablelands

Lumholtz's Tree-kangaroo is one of Australia's few marsupials that are active during the day as well as the night. It is a solitary animal that limits its social interactions to short mating interludes and occasional fights between males, but relationships between mothers and young are close.

The Lumholtz's Tree-roo is often seen at dawn and dusk.

These animals prefer to live in forests on fertile soil at high altitudes. Their primary habitat is the rainforest and occasionally the neighbouring wet sclerophyll forests of Far North Queensland's Atherton and Evelyn Tablelands. Spending the majority of their time in trees, they come down to travel on the ground—sometimes fair distances—between rainforest patches. Their favourite foods are rainforest leaves but rarely they will eat fruits and flowers.

With a face like a teddy bear, who can resist this tree-dwelling roo?

> **FAITHFUL TO THEIR PATCH**
> Even when Lumholtz's habitats are disturbed or destroyed, the animals do not move. This leaves them exposed and vulnerable to predators and starvation.

The population of Lumholtz's Tree-kangaroo is believed to be between ten and twenty thousand.

Bennett's Tree-kangaroo

This tree-roo is larger than its close relative, Lumholtz's Tree-kangaroo. It weighs 8–13.5kg and measures 70–75cm, with a 73–83cm tail. Bennett's has a light muzzle and a grey face with a reddish band around the ears, under the chin and onto the shoulders. The mostly greyish brown body has a black underside and caramel-coloured tail, black at its bushy tip.

Bennett's Tree-kangaroo is slightly larger than Lumholtz's, making it Australia's biggest tree-dwelling mammal. Its diet consists of leaves from a few tree and vine species as well as some fruit.

The elusive Bennett's Tree-kangaroo lives high in the tops of rainforest trees and is rarely seen.

Seldom Seen

Bennett's Tree-kangaroo, like Lumholtz's, appears to be primarily nocturnal but it is also active during the day. It is rarely seen because it is a wary animal and mostly lives at the top of tall trees, where it is extremely hard to see against the leafy canopy. Also, unlike Lumholtz's Tree-kangaroos that live on the Atherton and Evelyn Tablelands, Bennett's Tree-kangaroos live in a region not commonly visited by tourists: an area of only 2000 sq km of lowland vine forest and mountain rainforest in Far North Queensland.

> **POLYGAMY RULES**
> As is common practice among macropods, male tree-kangaroos will mate with more than one female.

Defending Territories

In these remote areas a male Bennett's Tree-kangaroo may defend a territory as large as 25 hectares. His home range will overlap that of several females but never that of another male. Should a neighbouring male trespass into another male's territory he could find himself embroiled in a ferocious fight as the guardian male protects what he considers his own.

A Checklist of Australian Macropods

Listed below are all 49 Australian species of
kangaroos and wallabies with their scientific and
family names. Forty-five are alive today; four have
become extinct since the arrival of Europeans.

FAMILY MACROPODIDAE

Eastern Grey Kangaroo *Macropus giganteus*
Western Grey Kangaroo *M. fuliginosus*
Red Kangaroo *M. rufus*
Common Wallaroo *M. robustus*
Antilopine Wallaroo *M. antilopinus*
Black Wallaroo *M. bernardus*

Agile Wallaby *M. agilis*
Tammar Wallaby *M. eugenii*
Black-striped Wallaby *M. dorsalis*
Red-necked Wallaby *M. rufogriseus*
Western Brush Wallaby *M. irma*
Parma Wallaby *M. parma*
Whiptail Wallaby *M. parryi*

Bridled Nailtail Wallaby *Onychogalea fraenata*
Northern Nailtail Wallaby *O. unguifera*

Swamp Wallaby *Wallabia bicolor*

Quokka *Setonix brachyurus*

Allied Rock-wallaby *Petrogale assimilis*
Short-eared Rock-wallaby *P. brachyotis*
Monjon *P. burbidgei*
Cape York Rock-wallaby *P. coenensis*
Nabarlek *P. concinna*
Godman's Rock-wallaby *P. godmani*
Herbert's Rock-wallaby *P. herberti*
Unadorned Rock-wallaby *P. inornata*
Black-footed Rock-wallaby *P. lateralis*
Mareeba Rock-wallaby *P. mareeba*
Brush-tailed Rock-wallaby *P. penicillata*
Proserpine Rock-wallaby *P. persephone*
Purple-necked Rock-wallaby *P. purpureicollis*
Rothschild's Rock-wallaby *P. rothschildi*
Sharman's Rock-wallaby *P. sharmani*
Yellow-footed Rock-wallaby *P. xanthopus*

Spectacled Hare-wallaby *Lagorchestes conspicillatus*
Rufous Hare-wallaby *L. hirsutus*

Banded Hare-wallaby *Lagostrophus fasciatus*

Tasmanian Pademelon *Thylogale billardierii*
Red-legged Pademelon *T. stigmatica*
Red-necked Pademelon *T. thetis*

Bennett's Tree-kangaroo *Dendrolagus bennettianus*
Lumholtz's Tree-kangaroo *D. lumholtzi*

Extinct
Toolache Wallaby *Macropus greyi*
Crescent Nailtail Wallaby *Onychogalea lunata*
Eastern Hare-wallaby *Lagorchestes leporides*
Central Hare-wallaby *Lagorchestes asomatus*

INDEX